A SOUND, DISCIPLINED MIND

Nancy Dufresne

DUFRESNE MINISTRIES
PUBLICATIONS

A Sound, Disciplined Mind
ISBN: 978-0-940763-35-7
Copyright © 2011, 2018, 2022, 2024 by Dufresne Ministries

Published by:
Dufresne Ministries Publications
P.O. Box 1010
Murrieta, CA 92564
www.dufresneministries.org

1-5000 2-2500 3-2500 4-3000 5-7500

Unless otherwise indicated, all Scriptural quotations are from the *King James Version* of the Bible.

Scripture quotations marked AMPC are taken from the *Amplified® Bible, Classic Edition (AMPC),* Copyright © 1954, 1958, 1962, 1964, 1965, 1987 by The Lockman Foundation. Used by permission. www.Lockman.org

Printed in the United States of America. All rights reserved under International Copyright Law. Contents and/or cover may not be reproduced in whole or in part in any form without the express consent of the publisher.

Cover design: Nancy Dufresne & Grant Dufresne

WORLD HARVEST
BIBLE TRAINING CENTER

M U R R I E T A · C A L I F O R N I A

TRAINING BELIEVERS TO MOVE WITH THE WORD & THE SPIRIT

FOR MORE INFO OR TO SUBMIT AN APPLICATION ONLINE, GO TO

WWW.WHBTC.ORG

OR CONTACT OUR OFFICE AT (951) 696-9258, EXT. 202

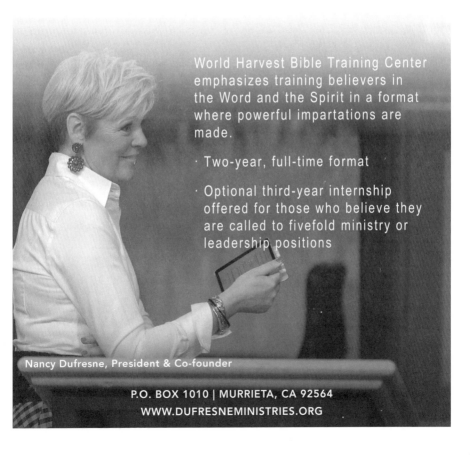

World Harvest Bible Training Center emphasizes training believers in the Word and the Spirit in a format where powerful impartations are made.

- Two-year, full-time format

- Optional third-year internship offered for those who believe they are called to fivefold ministry or leadership positions

Nancy Dufresne, President & Co-founder

P.O. BOX 1010 | MURRIETA, CA 92564
WWW.DUFRESNEMINISTRIES.ORG

Books by Nancy Dufresne

Daily Healing Bread From God's Table

His Presence Shall Be My Dwelling Place

The Healer Divine

Victory in the Name

*There Came a Sound From Heaven:
The Life Story of Dr. Ed Dufresne*

Visitations From God

Responding to the Holy Spirit

God: The Revealer of Secrets

A Supernatural Prayer Life

Causes

I Have a Supply

*Fit for the Master's Use:
A Handbook for Raising Godly Children*

Knowing Your Measure of Faith

The Greatness of God's Power

Peace: Living Free From Worry

Following the Holy Spirit

*An Apostle of the Anointing:
A Biography of Dr. Ed Dufresne*

Victory Over Grief & Sorrow

Answer It!

The Price of the Double Portion Anointing

Worship

Love: The Great Quest

Books in Spanish

Pan Diario de Sanidad de la Mesa de Dios
(Spanish edition of *Daily Healing Bread*)

Contents

Introduction ix
1. Renewing Your Mind 11
2. Exercising Your Authority 31
3. Don't Be Swayed 41
4. A Disciplined Mind 51
5. Free From Worry 71
6. Free From Fear 87
7. Keep Out Doubt 93
8. Freedom From Depression – The Praise Cure 99
9. No Condemnation – Forget It! 107
10. The Other Side of the Test 117
11. Count It All Joy 123
12. A Disciplined Mind in Prayer 131
13. Perfect Peace 139
Prayer of Salvation 143
How To Be Filled With the Holy Spirit 145
Prayer To Receive the Holy Spirit 149

Introduction

God offers you His thoughts – take them! They will transform you! God's Word is the thoughts of God written down so that you can make them your own. His words lived will reach into your everyday life, transforming it into something spiritual, supernatural, and extraordinary. There's nothing ordinary about the man who makes God's thoughts his own, for they will transform him and lift him out of the commonplace and into the supernatural – producing a life that bears much fruit and glorifies God; that man will become one who manifests God's will everywhere he goes, and he will aid in lifting others.

How do we make God's thoughts our own? By doing as God instructed Joshua:

> **JOSHUA 1:8 (AMPC)**
> **This Book of the Law shall not depart out of your mouth, but you shall MEDITATE on it DAY AND NIGHT, that you may observe and DO according to all that is written in it. For then you shall make your way prosperous, and then you shall deal wisely and have good success.**

As you daily meditate on God's Word, muttering it to yourself and thinking deeply into it, act on that Word, and talk to God about His Word, your mind will be renewed and your life will be transformed – it will become something different than it's ever been before.

Meditating on God's Word puts you in the verse and puts the verse in you, making it alive in you.

In the above verse, God is not mentioned and the devil is not mentioned. What is mentioned is God's Word and you! In fact, "you" are mentioned five times. So what determines your success in this life is what you do with the Word. Take God's Word and make it your own; make God's thoughts your thoughts and His ways your ways.

No, this process won't happen overnight, but as you meditate on God's Word day and night, making it a lifestyle, and as you make God's thoughts your own and act on His Word, you will experience all that God has made yours.

Let us turn away from thoughts not worthy of God, for neither are they worthy of His children.

Chapter 1

Renewing Your Mind

Our lives will equal our thought lives – good or bad. To improve our lives, we must improve our thought lives. God has given us the means whereby we can improve our thought lives – through renewing our minds with the Word of God, which will transform our lives. So the responsibility rests with us, not with God, to renew our minds. We must take God's Word and renew our minds, disciplining our minds to think in line with His Word. A renewed mind is a disciplined mind – disciplined to take on the thoughts of the Word.

"And be not conformed to this world: BUT BE YE TRANSFORMED BY THE RENEWING OF YOUR MIND, that ye may prove (discern) *what is that good, and acceptable, and perfect, will of God"* (Rom. 12:2). When you renew your mind with the Word of God, this verse says that it will transform your life; your life won't look the same or be the same. Those who are renewing their minds with the Word of God will live transformed lives. A transformed life will be able to accomplish what it couldn't accomplish before it was transformed.

Present Your Body to God

You are a threefold being: you are a spirit, you possess a soul (made up of your mind, will, and emotions), and you live in a body. At the time you were born again, God did something with your spirit – He took out that old spirit and nature of death that was in you, and He gave you a new spirit that now has the life and nature of God in it. But you still have the same mind and the same body you did before you were born again. Although God gave you a new spirit, the Word says that you are the one who has to do something with your mind and with your body.

What are you to do with your body? Paul tells us in Romans 12:1, *"...present your bodies a living sacrifice, holy, acceptable unto God, which is your reasonable service."* The Amplified Classic Bible reads, *"...which is your...spiritual worship."* You are to present your body to God to do that which glorifies Him. When you present your body to God to do that which is right in His sight, that is spiritual worship – that is one way you worship Him. To present your body to God is spiritual worship because it is something that you do with your spirit; with your spirit you present your body to God for His glory.

Paul also stated in 1 Corinthians 9:27, *"But I KEEP UNDER MY BODY, and bring it into subjection: lest that by any means, when I have preached to others, I myself should be a castaway* (or as another translation states, be disqualified).*"* Paul told us that he did something with his body – he kept it under. This apostle who was used to write a large portion of the New Testament still had to do something with his body; his body still wanted to do wrong, but he didn't let his body rule him – he kept it under. He didn't allow his body to rule him and do wrong. Paul said he kept his body under so that he wouldn't be a castaway or be disqualified.

Paul stated, *"But I keep under my body, and bring it into subjection...."* What did he bring his body in subjection to? He brought his body in subjection to his born-again spirit. He kept his body under the dominion of his own spirit. In other words, he let his spirit rule him, not his body. Your flesh will still want to do wrong, even though you're born again, but you have to keep it under.

As you spend time with God through feeding on His Word and in prayer, and as you act on that Word in your daily life, your spirit will be strengthened and developed. As you strengthen and develop your spirit, then it will be stronger than your flesh and you'll be able to keep your flesh under the dominion of your own spirit; you'll keep your flesh from dominating your life.

Romans 8:13 also tells us that, *"... ye through the Spirit do mortify the deeds of the body...."* If you will take time every day to speak in other tongues, your spirit will be strengthened and it will help you keep the body under – it will help you mortify or deaden the deeds of the body. Through the Spirit, or by speaking in other tongues, your spirit is built up, charged up, and strengthened to stay in dominion over your flesh.

A New Way of Thinking

Not only do you have to do something with your body, but you are the one who must do something with your mind – you must renew it with the Word of God. Paul told us, *"And be not conformed to this world: but be ye TRANSFORMED BY THE RENEWING OF YOUR MIND...."* To renew your mind is to give your mind a new way of thinking. When you renew your mind with the Word of God, you're taking God's thoughts and making them your own. You're replacing the old way you used to think with how God thinks. God's Word is God's thoughts. By feeding on and acting on God's Word, you're renewing your mind. To renew your mind is to give your mind new definitions – God's definitions, instead of human, natural definitions. When human, natural definitions and thinking are in opposition to what God's Word says, then lay natural thinking aside and take on the thoughts of the Word.

The unrenewed mind, the carnal mind, will reason against, argue, and struggle against the Word, but the renewed mind will agree with God's Word.

Faith is of the heart; you believe God with your heart – your spirit – not your mind. But the mind is to be renewed, for then it will agree with the Word and the faith that's in your heart and not oppose, argue, or struggle against it. The mind can be renewed to think faith thoughts. As my spiritual father stated, "A spiritual giant is one whose heart and mind agree."

To renew your mind with the Word of God is a process. It can't be done overnight, but as you daily renew your mind with the Word of God, your life will be transformed; your thoughts can be brought in line with God's thoughts. This is a process that must be carried out every day of your life for the rest of your life. The renewing of your mind is to be a life-long occupation. As one minister stated, "Your mind doesn't stay renewed any more than your hair stays combed." In other words, just as you must daily comb your hair to put it in place, you must daily renew your mind to keep your mind in line with His Word.

Right Thinking

As you renew your mind with God's Word, you replace wrong thinking with right thinking. Wrong thinking leads to wrong believing, wrong believing leads to wrong speaking, and wrong speaking opens the door for wrong things to happen. When you think wrong, believe wrong, or speak wrong, you give place to the devil. But as you renew your mind with the Word, you change wrong thinking to right thinking. When you have right thinking, then you'll have right believing and right speaking, and you will keep the door closed to the enemy.

Renewing your mind with the Word of God will be one of your mightiest defenses against the enemy, for correct knowledge of the Word will safeguard you from wrong thinking, wrong believing, and wrong speaking, and then his devices and strategies won't work against you. Renew your mind with the Word of God, for it will help you to keep the door closed to the enemy.

Gain Knowledge of the Word

By renewing your mind with the Word of God, you keep yourself from being ignorant of your rights and privileges in Christ, and then the devil can't take advantage of you. The devil thrives on ignorance. He's counting on ignorance to work his plan. The devil works in the earth through ignorance, but God works in the earth through knowledge. Hosea 4:6 tells us, *"My people are destroyed for lack of knowledge...."* The word "destroyed" means cut off. God's people are cut off from blessings through the lack of knowledge of God's Word. By renewing your mind, you protect yourself from failure that comes from ignorance of God's Word.

To receive what you need from God, you have to gain knowledge of how He works; that knowledge comes through the Word. When you cooperate with God by acting on His Word, then you will receive. That's why it's so important to renew your mind with the Word of God.

It's only through renewing your mind with the Word of God that you can know your rights and privileges in Christ and can experience victory in every arena of life.

The Saving of Your Soul

James wrote a letter and instructed the brethren to, *"...receive with meekness the engrafted word, which is able to SAVE YOUR SOULS"* (James 1:21). James was telling these Christians that their souls weren't saved. Yes, their spirits were born again and saved, but their souls (which are made up of the mind, the will, and the emotions) were still unsaved. He was telling them that they still had to renew their minds with the Word of God.

The Apostle John wrote in his letter, *"Beloved, I wish above all things that thou mayest prosper and be in health, EVEN AS THY SOUL PROSPERETH"* (3 John 1:2). John was letting these believers know that their prosperity and health were directly related to the prospering of their souls, the renewing of their minds. As they renewed their minds with the Word of God, they were causing their souls to prosper, which would cause the other arenas of their life to prosper.

David wrote in Psalm 23:1-3, *"The Lord is my shepherd; I shall not want. He maketh me to lie down in green pastures: he leadeth me beside the still waters. HE RESTORETH MY SOUL...."* How does God restore your soul? Through the Word of God. As you feed and act on the Word of God, your soul is restored.

As we can see in these passages, Paul calls this process the "renewing of the mind." James calls it the "saving of your soul." John calls it the "prospering of the soul." David calls it the "restoring of the soul." They are all saying the same thing. To experience success in life, you must take time to renew your mind with the Word. This happens as you feed on God's Word in your private devotional time and as you sit under accurate teaching of the Word.

It's not enough to *know* what the Word says – you must be a *doer* of the Word if your mind is to be renewed.

The Restoration Process

My mother loved to restore antique furniture. She got thrilled when she found a beautiful piece of furniture that needed restoring, for she could see its potential past the old, damaged finish; she was expectant about what it could become. A beautiful piece was made even more beautiful after it was restored. Even a piece of furniture that seemingly had no apparent beauty could be brought to a place of great beauty once it was restored.

Even so, as a believer renews his mind with the Word of God, God is able to restore his mind, and his life will be transformed until it becomes a life of great beauty – a life that moves with God.

When Mother acquired a piece of furniture that was in desperate need of restoration, with great expectation she laid out all the supplies and tools necessary to help bring about and complete the restoration process. Although it required much work and great effort, she knew it was worth it, for she knew the rewards of the outcome.

Expectantly she collected and laid out her supplies – sand paper, paint stripper, scraping tools, and grinder – all things necessary for the work. As she began, she applied much effort in stripping and sanding the wood, digging in the corners to remove the build-up, and if necessary, even the power grinder was put to use. As she undertook her great task, no effort was spared to do the job right, for she knew that without this process that piece of furniture would never have been all it could be.

Likewise, the restoring of the mind is a process that will require a putting forth of effort. It will require time, effort, and diligence to feed and meditate on God's Word. It will require an effort on your part to bring that Word into every thought and action of your daily life, but it's worth every effort; it is a joyous work! Don't shun that restoration process, that process of renewing your mind with the Word of God, for if you're faithful to it, your life will never be the same. It will push what may be wrong out of your mind and your life, and it will allow God's best to flow – it will transform you.

Realize that God values and loves you so much that He won't leave you as He found you. God's Word will reach into every part of your life and bring it in line with His Word and His plan; it only requires that God have your full agreement and cooperation. It's a thrilling, positive work. Let it be a thrill and a joy to you to submit yourself to the far-reaching effects of the Word; it will work mightily in you. Don't tire of or quit this divine work of renewing your mind with His Word, for if you're faithful to it, it will transform your life and you will experience all that God has provided for you.

Speed Up the Process

Your mind is renewed through feeding on the Word and through sitting under accurate teaching of the Word. The more you feed on God's Word and sit under the teaching of God's Word, the more your mind is renewed. You are the one who measures the rate of that restoration process to yourself by how much you feed on the Word, sit under the teaching of the Word, and act on the Word. To feed on the Word, but never act on it, never make it part of your daily life, will keep you in an unrenewed state. The renewed mind acts on the Word.

As my mother would restore an old piece of furniture, she would give as much attention and time as possible to the process. She would sometimes work late into the night. She knew it would only prolong the restoration process if she didn't give much time to it. But if she would give an all-out effort to it, giving all the time necessary to restore it, then she could start benefiting from the use of that furniture sooner.

Even so, there are great benefits to renewing your mind, and the more attention and time you give to it, the quicker you'll enjoy the benefits. If you only study or sit under the teaching of the Word occasionally, the renewing of your mind will be a slow process and progress won't be very evident. But if you will faithfully and diligently give time to the Word, you will speed up this wonderful restoration process and your life will show the fruit of it.

How do you renew your mind with God's Word? You feed on His Word, meditate on it (think deeply into, mutter it to yourself, and talk to God about His Word), and act on it, making it a part of your everyday life. You bring that Word into your daily thoughts and into your words and actions (Joshua 1:8).

Before you address a situation or a problem in your life, develop the habit of first asking yourself, *What does the Word say about this?* Then act in line with the Word.

You realize that the Bible is not only a book to be read, but it contains God's Words that are to be lived; they are instructions to you for your everyday life. It is God speaking to you. It is what you govern your life by. You are a doer of what the Word says.

Stay in the Arena of Faith

God leads us through our spirits, not through our minds or our bodies. Proverbs 20:27 tells us, *"The spirit of man is the candle of the Lord, searching all the inward parts of the belly."* This means that God is going to enlighten you through your spirit. When God speaks to you, He will speak to your spirit. What He says to your spirit will float up and enlighten your mind; it comes from your spirit within. But when the devil speaks to you, he speaks to your mind; his words come against your mind from the outside.

Since God leads us through our spirits, the more sensitive we are to our own spirits, and the more we follow our spirits, the more success we'll experience. We must develop, train, and educate our spirits. This is done by feeding and meditating on God's Word, by acting on God's Word, by fellowshipping with God in prayer, and by obeying what God says to our spirits. We become sensitive to our spirits and to the Spirit of God by taking time to speak in other tongues on a daily basis.

Not only does God lead and guide you through your spirit, but the faith of God is in your spirit, not in your mind. To stay hooked up to your spirit is to stay hooked up to the arena of faith. You stay in the arena of faith by letting your spirit take the lead, not your mind. You stay in the arena of faith by speaking God's Word from your spirit. As you stay in the arena of faith, you will overcome every opposition of the enemy. The enemy doesn't want you to stay in the faith arena; he wants to draw you out of the arena of faith, the spirit arena, into the mental arena, which is the realm of reason.

The mind is Satan's chief battleground. Your greatest battles will be in the mental arena. He attacks the mind to try to hold you in the mental arena and out of the spirit arena, which is the arena of faith. If the devil can hold you in the mental arena, he'll whip you. But if you hold him in the spirit arena, the arena of faith, you'll whip him. You hold him in the arena of faith by answering wrong thoughts with the Word of God from your spirit and then by praising God for His Word to hold your attention on God and off wrong thoughts.

Answer Wrong Thoughts With the Word

The greatest power the devil has is the power of suggestion. He will suggest a wrong thought to your mind, trying to get you to turn that thought over in your mind to make it part of your thought life. If that thought is allowed to become part of your thought life, it can unsettle and trouble you, but you can refuse to let wrong thoughts into your thought life. You keep those thoughts from entering your thought life by refusing to turn them over in your mind; refuse to think about them. Instead, answer those thoughts with the Word of God. Wrong thoughts will come, as they do to all of us, but they don't have to gain entrance into your thought life.

If you have allowed wrong thoughts into your thought life, you can close the door to those wrong thoughts. To overcome wrong thoughts that may have troubled or unsettled you, answer every wrong thought with the Word of God. Refuse to think on those wrong thoughts; refuse to turn them over in your mind. Instead, fill your mouth and your thought life with God's thoughts, God's Word. To fill your thought life with God's Word, think on what He says and praise Him for His Word, and the right thoughts and the right words will overcome and shut out the wrong thoughts.

You can't "out-think" wrong thoughts – you must answer them with the Word of God. Learn to answer and not entertain the suggestions and the wrong thoughts the enemy brings; don't touch them or turn them over in your thought life. Refuse to be disturbed by the thoughts the enemy brings; don't give him that kind of attention. Rather, hold fast to God's Word by keeping His words and praises to God in your mouth and in your thought life.

One strategy the enemy uses against the mind is repetition. He will suggest something over and over to the mind, but no matter how many times or how long he suggests it, resist it by answering it with the Word of God. Repetition doesn't make it true. Hold fast to God's Word and don't let any repeated suggestions of the enemy change your faith in the Word of God.

If you are to renew your mind with the Word of God, you must do as instructed in 2 Corinthians 10:5, *"CASTING DOWN IMAGINATIONS, and every high thing that exalteth itself against the knowledge of God, and bringing into captivity EVERY THOUGHT to the obedience of Christ."* As you are renewing your mind with God's Word, you must pay attention to the thoughts you allow yourself to think upon. If a thought isn't in line with God's Word, you must cast it down and replace it with thoughts of the Word. Cast down all wrong imaginations, including those that depict the worst happening. You must make certain that every thought is in line with God's Word; if it's not, you must not allow it into your thought life.

One who is renewing his mind with the Word of God disciplines and closely guards his thought life. As one minister stated, "You can't keep the birds from flying around your head, but you can keep them from building a nest in your hair." Wrong thoughts come to everyone; you can't keep wrong thoughts from coming to you, but you can keep them from becoming part of your thought life by refusing to turn those thoughts over in your mind. Instead, quiet your mind, and from your spirit answer wrong thoughts with the Word of God, then praise God to hold your attention on God and His Word and off wrong thoughts.

Grow in Peace

As you feed on God's Word, your knowledge of the Word will grow and you will quickly recognize thoughts that are not in line with His Word. As you feed on God's Word, you will grow in your understanding of what belongs to you because you are in Christ. When you understand who you are in Christ and take your place in Christ, exercising your authority over the enemy and over the thoughts the enemy suggests, refusing to allow them into your thought life, peace will be the flow of your life.

Peter wrote, *"Grace and PEACE BE MULTIPLIED UNTO YOU through the KNOWLEDGE of God, and of Jesus our Lord"* (2 Peter 1:2). As your knowledge of the Word grows, so does peace. To grow in peace, grow in your knowledge of the Word and be a doer of the Word.

Fill Up With the Water of the Word

In a house we used to live in, I would put the water bowl for our dogs by the garage door, where there happened to be a light. At night time, all the moths and bugs would be flying around that light, but in the morning, those bugs would be floating in the dog's water. I wouldn't touch those bugs to pull them out of the water; I would just get the water hose and turn on the water. I would fill up the bowl with water, and the bugs would just float off.

Likewise, you don't have to try to pick the wrong thoughts out of your mind. Just turn on the water of the Word. If thoughts try to trouble you, you don't have to struggle, trying to "get rid" of them – just turn on the water of the Word. Fill your thoughts and your mouth with what God says. Turn your attention toward the Word and away from wrong thoughts; become occupied and absorbed with what God's Word says, and the wrong thoughts will just float off.

If I would have tried to pick those bugs out of the water myself, they would have fallen to pieces in the water and I would have made a bigger mess. Likewise, if you try to "out-think" or handle wrong thoughts mentally, struggling to get rid of them, trying to pick them out of your mind, you'll end up with a bigger mess. The more you handle them mentally, turning them over and over in your mind trying to "out-think" them or get rid of them, the more mindful you become of them and the more they seem to multiply.

We should not be trying to get rid of wrong and troubling thoughts, but rather, turn the mind to higher thoughts – God's thoughts – the thoughts of the Word. Taking God's thoughts will cause all lesser ones to lose sway, washing them from any place of influence. When these higher thoughts, the thoughts of the Word, are given their rightful place in our hearts, mouths, and thought life, they will bring about transformation. All lesser thoughts will be dismissed, and the fruit of God's thoughts will be great peace.

"GREAT PEACE have they which love thy law: and nothing shall offend them" (Ps. 119:165). One definition of the

word "offend" is to cause to stumble. So, we could correctly quote this verse saying, *"Great peace have they which love thy law; and nothing* (not even the accusations, suggestions, or thoughts of the enemy) *shall offend them* (or cause them to stumble)."

This verse tells us that those who love God's law, God's Word, will have great peace. We show our love for God's Word by doing it – holding to it at all times and in the face of all opposition. When we do, we will have great peace.

One can become so absorbed and occupied with the Word that all attention is drawn completely away from opposing thoughts. One's mind can become so full of and dominated by the flow of the Word that all lesser thoughts are washed out of the thought life.

When faced with wrong thoughts, rest and recline yourself on God's Word. Keep God's Word in your mouth and in your thoughts, and let the water of the Word do its work; it will wash the wrong thoughts away.

Give attention to renewing your mind, and as you do, the outcome will be transforming – it will transform your life.

The Local Church

Our minds are renewed as we feed on the Word of God in our own study time and as we sit under accurate teaching of God's Word. The primary place we are taught God's Word is in the local church. That's one reason the local church is of such great and vital importance in the life of the believer; it's one of the few places where we can receive the Word of God that renews the mind.

The Spirit of God will direct us to a church to attend – one that teaches and preaches the Word – and it's important that we follow the Spirit's leading, for that church will be vital in the process of renewing our minds.

We are to be thrilled that we are able to have our minds renewed. Since the local church that teaches and preaches the Word is part of that process, then we should be thrilled to attend church services.

The enemy will use every strategy he can to keep you away from a church that teaches God's Word, for he wants to hinder or interrupt the process of renewing your mind. He doesn't want you to gain knowledge of God's Word. He wants to hold people in ignorance so he can work unhindered. In an attempt to draw you away from church, the enemy will try to use a busy schedule, offense, unforgiveness, strife, or a host of other devices.

If he can't keep you out of church, then he'll try to use distractions during a service to draw your attention away from receiving the Word that is being taught. But discipline your mind so that while the teaching or preaching of the Word is going on in a service, you don't allow yourself to be distracted and miss hearing your answer, which is the Word of God. The Word is your answer – don't be distracted from it.

Each of us should hold the highest regard for our pastor who feeds us the Word of God, for they help us to renew our minds with God's Word. They, along with the other fivefold offices, play a vital role in feeding us the Word that renews our minds. That's one reason we are to honor and respect the supply they bring to our lives. We are to protect our relationship with our pastor and protect their role in our lives, for their supply is crucial to our spiritual development. We are not to allow wrong thoughts or wrong things to separate us from the pastor God puts in our lives, because we need the supply they bring.

Honoring the office of the pastor and the local church is important because the local church is a place where you are fed the Word that renews the mind. That's one reason church services should be the highlight of your week – teach that to your children. Come to church ready to receive! Come expecting! Be thrilled to sit under God's Word, for as you respond to God and His Word, it will transform your life!

Chapter 2

Exercising Your Authority

The mind is the devil's primary battleground. He attacks you in the mental arena in an attempt to hold you in the mental arena, for that's his arena. If he can hold you in the mental arena, he'll whip you. But you are to hold him in the arena of faith. If you hold him in the arena of faith – the arena of the spirit, then you'll whip him. You hold him in the arena of faith by answering wrong thoughts with the Word of God and then by praising God for His Word.

When Jesus was in the wilderness being tempted of the devil for forty days and forty nights, He answered every temptation with, *"It is written..."* (Luke 4). Jesus overcame every temptation by answering the enemy with the Word of God. Jesus' policy of dealing with the devil was to answer him with, "It is written."

You must learn how to answer the devil. Answer him with the Word of God. You can't out-think him – answer him with God's Word in your mouth.

The enemy wants to capture your thought life, so he seeks to inject thoughts. The only power the enemy has is the power of suggestion. He will suggest a thought, and if he can get you to continually turn it over in your thought life, then you could start believing it. If you believe it, then you'll speak it, and you'll open the door to him.

But as a child of God, you have total and absolute authority over him! As you stand your ground against him and resist the thoughts he brings, he will flee from you. James 4:7 tells us, *"Submit yourselves therefore to God. Resist the devil, and he will flee from you."* We're not resisting him in ourselves; we are resisting him as one who is in Christ – one who has been given authority over him.

You Have Authority

Jesus defeated Satan and stripped him, leaving him utterly defeated. Colossians 2:15 tells us, *"And having spoiled principalities and powers, he made a shew of them openly, triumphing over them in it."* Other translations of this verse state that Satan and all evil spirits were utterly defeated; they were brought to naught and reduced to nothing.

Paul told us in Colossians 1:13 that God, *"...hath delivered us from the power* (authority) *of darkness, and hath translated us into the kingdom of his dear Son."* We are no longer under Satan's authority and dominion; he has been stripped of his power to harm us. We are now under the authority of God's Kingdom. Jesus defeated Satan, but He didn't do it for Himself – He did it for us. We don't resist Satan based on anything we've done, but based on what Jesus did for us. When He defeated and stripped Satan of his authority to harm us, He handed us the victory He won.

Jesus said, *"Behold, I give unto you power* (authority) *to tread on serpents and scorpions, and over all the power of the enemy: and nothing shall by any means hurt you"* (Luke 10:19). Jesus is telling us that we are the ones with the authority over the enemy. If he opposes us, we are to exercise our authority over him – we are to resist him.

Jesus also told us in Matthew 16:19, *"And I will give unto thee the keys of the kingdom of heaven: and whatsoever thou shalt bind on earth shall be bound in heaven: and whatsoever thou shalt loose on earth shall be loosed in heaven."* We have dominion and authority. Heaven operates by exercising authority. Jesus says that now we have that same authority over our lives on this earth. Whatsoever we bind shall be bound. Whatsoever we loose shall be loosed, and Heaven will back us up.

Matthew 16:19 says, *"...whatsoever thou shalt bind on earth shall be bound IN HEAVEN: and whatsoever thou shalt loose on earth shall be loosed IN HEAVEN."* Does anything need to be bound in Heaven, or does anything need to be loosed in Heaven? Not in the Heaven where God is. The Bible speaks of three heavens (2 Cor. 12:2). The first heaven is the atmospheric heaven that's around the earth, the second heaven is where the great solar systems and galaxies lie, and the third heaven is where God is. So, when we exercise our authority to bind or loose, the heaven that's affected is the first heaven, for in the atmospheric heaven around the earth is where there is demon activity.

In 2 Corinthians 4:4, Satan is called the god of this world. How did he get to be the god of this world? Adam originally had the authority over the earth, for in Genesis 1:28 God told man to subdue the earth and to have dominion. But when Adam disobeyed God and sinned, committing high treason against God, he turned over his authority upon the earth to the one he obeyed – Satan; that's how Satan became the god of this world. But when Jesus defeated Satan, He restored that authority back to the Church, the Body of Christ. Satan no longer has any authority over us.

Seated Far Above

COLOSSIANS 2:15
And having spoiled principalities and powers, he made a shew of them openly, triumphing over them in it.

(AMPC)
[God] disarmed the principalities and powers that were ranged against us and made a bold display and public example of them, in triumphing over them in Him and in it [the cross].

EPHESIANS 1:20-23
20 ...he raised him from the dead, and set him at his own right hand in the heavenly places,

**21 Far above all principality, and power, and might, and dominion, and every name that is named, not only in this world, but also in that which is to come:
22 And hath put all things under his feet, and gave him to be the head over all things to the church,
23 Which is his body, the fulness of him that filleth all in all.**

**EPHESIANS 2:4-6
4 But God, who is rich in mercy, for his great love wherewith he loved us,
5 Even when we were dead in sins, hath quickened us together with Christ, (by grace ye are saved;)
6 And hath raised us up together, and made us sit together in heavenly places in Christ Jesus.**

God raised Jesus from the dead and set Him at His own right hand, *far above* every evil power, principality, might and dominion; all these evil powers opposed Him being raised, but to no avail – they were utterly defeated.

Not only did God raise up Jesus, but He also raised *us* up together with Him, and made us, the Church, to sit together with Christ in heavenly places; it is a seat of victory and authority. The authority we exercise is an authority that stems from the Throne. We occupy a seat that is *far above* all evil powers. The devil and evil spirits have no authority over the believer, for we have been delivered from the authority of the enemy and translated into God's Kingdom, and every believer now has joint seating with Christ *far above* all our enemies.

As we renew our minds with the truth of these scriptures, we see that we are no victim to the enemy. Because of what Jesus did for us, we are made to reign in this life.

> **ROMANS 5:17**
> **For if by one man's offence** (Adam's sin) **death reigned by one; much more they which receive abundance of grace and of the gift of righteousness SHALL REIGN IN LIFE by one, Jesus Christ.**

We are to reign over circumstances in this life; they are not to reign over us.

You must exercise your authority over the enemy if you are to reign over circumstances.

The enemy will oppose you over this subject of your authority; he doesn't want you to gain knowledge of your authority over him, and he doesn't want you to exercise your authority. He will oppose you to try to make you think your authority doesn't work and to try to back you down from using your authority. Once you successfully stand your ground against the enemy in one arena, he will still seek to gain entrance by attacking you in a different arena. But no matter what the opposition, continue to exercise your authority and stand your ground. Don't let his opposition stop you from exercising your authority – that's why he comes against you, but we're not ignorant of this strategy he uses.

In every encounter with the enemy, always remember that he is defeated, the victory is yours, and you are seated *far above* all your enemies.

The Wisdom of God

"But of him are ye in Christ Jesus, who of God is made unto us wisdom..." (1 Cor. 1:30). The wisdom that God gives you is to reveal to you who you are in Christ, the authority that is yours in Christ, and that Jesus' defeat of the enemy is complete. You don't have to fight the devil; you don't have to defeat him, for Jesus already defeated him for you. You are to fight only one fight – the good fight of faith. Paul wrote, *"Fight the good fight of faith..."* (1 Tim. 6:12), which means to stand your ground on God's Word. Remind the enemy that he's defeated and that he has no authority over you. You don't have to get victory – Jesus already got it for you. Boldly confess that victory is yours, and stand your ground on the Word, refusing to be swayed. Every time the enemy opposes you, exercise your authority over him.

You're in Authority

Some Christians go through certain tests because they didn't stand their ground against the devil and exercise their authority over him. By failing to take a stand against the enemy, the door was opened to the enemy and the enemy took advantage of them. If the door was opened to the enemy by failing to exercise authority over him, then the door can be closed to the enemy by exercising authority over him.

Some who are facing difficulties are waiting for God to do something about their problem when God has already authorized them to take a stand against the devil and put him on the run (Luke 10:19; 1 Peter 5:8 & 9). If they don't exercise their authority over the enemy, nothing will be done on their behalf, for Jesus gave the believer authority over the devil.

Still others are counting on the faith and the prayers of others to pull them through their difficulties, but any help that may come through the faith and prayers of others will only be temporary. They will still have to exercise their authority over the enemy for themselves to *maintain* any victory they received with the help of someone else's prayers and someone else's faith.

Prayer is important and has its place, but praying or having others pray for you is no substitute for you taking a bold stand on the Word and resisting the enemy for yourself.

When the enemy opposes you, resist him in Jesus' Name and boldly confess God's Word.

Exercise Yourself in Faith and Authority

Men who become spiritual giants and have a great effect on this earth are men of faith who walk in their authority. Smith Wigglesworth was such a man. He was an English preacher who had a powerful healing and miracle ministry during the early 1900s. He said that every day he exercised himself in faith and authority. Every day he released his faith through his words and actions, and he exercised his authority over circumstances and over the enemy every time the devil opposed him.

Jesus' victory over the enemy was total and complete, and your victory over him is total and complete. Renew your mind with these truths of God's Word, exercise your faith and authority, and you will reign over circumstances in this life.

When the enemy sends thoughts against the mind, whether they're thoughts of doubt, fear, or anything that's negative, you have authority over them. Resist wrong thoughts, resist the devil in Jesus' Name, and he will flee. Don't be mindful of the enemy and what he tries to do. Rather, be mindful of the Word. Be mindful of your position of authority and the victory that is yours in Christ. *Don't allow your mind to touch on anything except victory.*

Chapter 3

Don't Be Swayed

Finally, my brethren, be strong in the Lord, and in the power of his might.

Put on the whole armour of God, that ye may be able to stand against the wiles of the devil.

For we wrestle not against flesh and blood, but against principalities, against powers, against the rulers of the darkness of this world, against spiritual wickedness in high places.

— Ephesians 6:10-12

Full of the Word

We are told to "be strong in the Lord." We're not told to be strong in ourselves, but we're to be strong "in the Lord." What does it mean to "be strong in the Lord?" God and His Word are one. To be strong in the Lord means to be strong in the Word. Colossians 3:16 instructs us, *"Let the word of Christ dwell in you RICHLY in all wisdom...."* Feed yourself on God's Word; put it in your heart and mind – fill yourself with the Word.

What you're full of is what will move you. The Bible tells us that Jesus was full of compassion for the multitudes and He healed them. The compassion He was full of moved Him to heal them.

Full of the Spirit

Ephesians 6:10 tells us to *"...be strong in the Lord, AND IN THE POWER OF HIS MIGHT."* We're to be strong in the Lord, and we're to be strong in the power of His might. What does it mean to be strong "in the power of His might?" The power of His might is the Holy Ghost. To "be strong in the power of His might" means to be *full* of the Spirit. If you're full of the Spirit, you'll be able to take a bold, strong stand against the enemy. You need to be full of the Word and full of the Spirit.

How are we to live full of the Spirit? Acts tells us,

> **ACTS 2:1-4**
> **1** And when the day of Pentecost was fully come, they were all with one accord in one place.
> **2** And suddenly there came a sound from heaven as of a rushing mighty wind, and it filled all the house where they were sitting.
> **3** And there appeared unto them cloven tongues like as of fire, and it sat upon each of them.
> **4** And they were all **FILLED WITH THE HOLY GHOST, AND BEGAN TO SPEAK WITH OTHER TONGUES,** as the Spirit gave them utterance.

When the disciples were initially filled with the Spirit, they began to speak with other tongues.

Acts also records what happened when the disciples were again assembled together at a later time.

> **ACTS 4:31**
> **And when they had prayed, the place was shaken where they were assembled together; and THEY WERE ALL FILLED WITH THE HOLY GHOST, and they spake the word of God with boldness.**

This shows us that although the disciples had been initially filled with the Holy Ghost on the Day of Pentecost, they also received subsequent infillings.

Ephesians 5:18 instructs us, *"And be not drunk with wine, wherein is excess; but BE FILLED with the Spirit."* The original Greek text (the New Testament was originally written in Greek) reads, *"...BE BEING FILLED with the Spirit...,"* which shows an ongoing action. We are to "be being filled with the Spirit" for the rest of our lives. We are not trying to maintain yesterday's infilling, but we are to receive a fresh infilling every day; we are to continually be filled.

How are we to live full of the Spirit? When the disciples were initially filled with the Spirit, they began to speak with other tongues. So, one way to continue to be filled with the Spirit is to keep speaking with other tongues.

To be filled with the Spirit and to speak with other tongues is one of the greatest privileges of the believer. As you speak with other tongues, you build and charge yourself up on your most holy faith (Jude 20). As you speak with other tongues, your spirit is communicating directly with God (1 Cor. 14:2). Speaking with other tongues is one way to continue to be filled with the Holy Ghost. (To be filled with the Holy Ghost with the evidence of speaking in other tongues, see the chapter on "How To Be Filled With the Holy Spirit.")

Paul instructs us,

> **EPHESIANS 5:18-20**
> **18 And be not drunk with wine, wherein is excess; but BE FILLED with the Spirit;**
> **19 Speaking to yourselves in psalms and hymns and spiritual songs, singing and making melody in your heart to the Lord;**
> **20 Giving thanks always for all things unto God and the Father in the name of our Lord Jesus Christ.**

Another way to continue to be filled with the Spirit is to speak to ourselves in psalms, hymns, and spiritual songs in our daily lives.

One definition of the word *psalm* is a sacred song or poem. It can be sung or spoken. We have 150 of these recorded in the Old Testament book of Psalms. A *hymn* is a song of praise. A *spiritual song* is a song given by the Spirit of God that holds revelation of the Word. Psalms, hymns, and spiritual songs are not songs one might sing out of a songbook, but they are fresh from Heaven, given by the Spirit of God. This is another way one may continue to be filled with the Spirit.

God's plan under the New Covenant is for every believer to be filled with the Holy Spirit, for that is an emphasis of the New Testament. Living full of the Spirit enriches our lives in many ways, which includes helping us to live a spirit-led life, where our spirits take the lead instead of being dominated by our minds or our bodies.

To be strong *"in the power of His might"* we must also have a strong, fervent prayer life, one that is based on the Word of God. James 5:16 tells us, *"...The earnest (heartfelt, continued) prayer of a righteous man makes TREMENDOUS POWER AVAILABLE [dynamic in its working]"* (AMPC). This kind of praying will cause the power of God to be made available, bringing it into manifestation. This kind of praying will help us to continue to be filled with the Spirit.

"To be strong in the Lord and in the power of His might" means to be strong in the Word and in the Spirit – to be full of the Word and the Spirit (Eph. 6:10). As we live full of the Word and the Spirit, we can stand strong against any opposition.

The Armor of God

Paul goes on to instruct us in Ephesians 6:11 to, *"Put on the whole armour of God, that ye may be able to stand against the wiles* (strategies) *of the devil."* In Ephesians 6:14-17 we have the armor of God listed:

1. *Girdle of truth* – to understand God's Word accurately.

2. *Breastplate of righteousness* – we are righteous, in right standing with God, because of our redemption in Christ. When we know we are right with God and right with the Word in the stance we are taking, then no matter what opposes us, we know we are on safe ground.

3. *Feet shod with the preparation of the gospel of peace* – daily walking in the light of the Word and being a doer of the Word.

4. *Shield of faith* – we quench every fiery dart of the enemy with the shield of faith in God's Word. The devil will send every kind of fiery dart against the mind, but faith in God's Word will quench it.

5. *Helmet of salvation* – knowledge of your position in God because of your redemption, which includes knowing who you are in Christ and your rights and privileges in Christ. It protects your mind from wrong thinking, which is the enemy's primary battleground.

6. *Sword of the Spirit, which is the Word of God* – this is using the spoken Word against the enemy. Answer his attacks by speaking the Word of God. All the other pieces of armor are defensive, but this is the only offensive weapon we have.

We must *continually* be arrayed in our spiritual armor. When we are dressed in the armor of God, we are equipped to overcome any attack of the enemy.

Don't Be Swayed

In Ephesians, Paul tells us,

EPHESIANS 6:12
For we wrestle not against flesh and blood, but against principalities, against powers, against the rulers of the darkness of this world, against spiritual wickedness in high places.

Many read the word "wrestle" and think that we're to wrestle with the enemy. But W. E. Vine's *Expository Dictionary of New Testament Words* says that the word "wrestle" means to sway. The wrestling we encounter is when the devil and evil spirits try to sway us. They try to sway us from standing our ground on God's Word. They try to sway us out of faith and into worry, fear, and doubt. They try to sway us out of the spirit and into the mental arena. But if we're full of the Word and the Spirit and fully clad in the armor of God, they can't sway us as we take a firm stand on God's Word.

During a test, the enemy may try to bombard your mind; he will try to pressure your mind in an attempt to sway you away from faith in God's Word. Answer those thoughts with the Word of God and refuse to be swayed.

The wrestling we do is not in wrestling against the devil – Jesus already defeated him; we're not to wrestle with a defeated foe. *The wrestling we do is to fight the good fight of faith, which is done by keeping our thoughts and mouths filled with the Word in the face of all opposition.* We hold fast to our faith in God's Word when everything is trying to sway us into doubt and unbelief.

Paul told Timothy to, *"Fight the good fight of faith..."* (1 Tim. 6:12). The good fight of faith is a fight of words. When you're fighting the good fight of faith, you're keeping the Word of God in your mouth in the face of all contradictory circumstances. The good fight of faith is the only fight the believer is to engage in. Speak words of faith and those words will do the fighting for you. The good fight of faith is a fight of words.

Stand Your Ground

I PETER 5:8 & 9 (AMPC)
8 Be well balanced (temperate, sober of mind), be vigilant and cautious at all times; for that enemy of yours, the devil, roams around like a lion roaring [in fierce hunger], seeking someone to seize upon and devour.
9 Withstand him; BE FIRM IN FAITH [against his onset – rooted, established, strong, immovable, and determined]....

We will have to be strong and immovable in our stand on God's Word, standing firm. We must stand our ground, no matter what the circumstances may be. We must refuse to be swayed by the devil and evil spirits or by circumstances.

Victory Is Ours

We can take a bold stand on God's Word because Jesus defeated Satan in our stead and then gave the victory to us. His victory became our victory; therefore, we have victory over the enemy. We're not trying to get the victory; the victory is ours already.

John tells us, *"...this is the victory that overcometh the world, even OUR FAITH"* (1 John 5:4). Your victory is waiting on your faith to show up. When you exercise your faith, you will experience the victory that Jesus made yours. Your faith activates the victory that is yours. Your faith is released as you speak and act on God's Word. Faith has to be released before you'll benefit from it.

Keep speaking God's Word in the face of all adverse circumstances; refuse to be swayed from God's Word. Hold fast to your confession of victory, regardless of circumstances, for victory is yours right in the face of opposition and in the presence of the enemy.

Chapter 4

A Disciplined Mind

For though we walk in the flesh, we do not war after the flesh:

(For the weapons of our warfare are not carnal, but mighty through God to the pulling down of strong holds;)

Casting down imaginations, and every high thing that exalteth itself against the knowledge of God, and bringing into captivity every thought to the obedience of Christ.
– 2 Corinthians 10:3-5

Notice the phrase "pulling down of strong holds." Many have a misunderstanding of what "strong holds" are, but verse 5 tells us what they are – they are wrong imaginations, thoughts, or reasonings that are contrary to the Word of God. Wrong ways of thinking are the "strong holds" that must be dealt with.

Ignorance of God's Word produces wrong thinking, and wrong thinking produces wrong believing. The devil thrives on ignorance; he's counting on ignorance to work his plan, for ignorance produces wrong thinking and wrong believing, which opens the door to the devil. Right thinking is thinking in line with the Word of God, and it will keep the door closed to the enemy.

People think wrong because they've never been taught the Word, have sat under incorrect teaching, or have formulated their own ideas and concepts about God and how He works. But the Word of God is the remedy for wrong thinking. No matter what you've thought or been taught in the past, dismiss and reject any thinking that isn't in line with God's Word. You must discipline your mind to only accept that which is in line with the Word of God. If it isn't in line with the Word, you must cast it down. Cast down all wrong imaginations, including those that depict the worst happening. You must bring every thought into captivity to the obedience of Christ.

Don't Believe All You Hear

As I stated earlier, the mind is Satan's chief battleground. He will suggest wrong thoughts to your mind, but you have full authority to resist them and cast them down.

You're going to hear the enemy talk; you're going to hear the suggestions and the threats the enemy makes. You can't stop the devil from talking, but then you must have something to say; answer him with the Word. Even though you will hear the enemy talk, you don't have to believe what he says – you don't have to listen to him. Don't become occupied with what the enemy says, for he's a liar, and his lies are to be rejected and resisted, not believed. Tell him that you refuse to believe his lies. Anything that's not in line with the Word of God is to be rejected.

When going through a test, you may feel the effects of that test on the mind and on the body. A test may try to apply great pressure to the mind, but we are not to walk by what we feel or see – we must walk by faith in God's Word.

"Where Is Your Faith?"

I remember a time of testing I went through years ago as a young Christian. During that time, thoughts came against my mind in a way I hadn't experienced before, and I handled it wrong. I kept trying to deal with those thoughts mentally, and as I did, they only held me in the mental arena. When troubling thoughts came, I should have resisted the devil by speaking the Word and then refused to listen to them or meditate on the thoughts that were coming to me, refusing to touch them in my thought life. But because I turned the thoughts over in my mind, I was held in the mental arena. I didn't stay in the spirit, which is the arena of faith, so the struggle continued.

I had just started preaching, and my husband and I were conducting meetings in a church during this time. I was scheduled to preach the Sunday morning service, but the last thing I wanted to do that morning was preach; I was having such a struggle. As I was sitting on the platform during the song service, all of a sudden, Jesus came up the side aisle, walked up the steps to the platform, and came and stood next to me. (I didn't see Jesus with my physical eyes. All of this happened by the word of knowledge. Although I didn't see Him, I knew exactly where He was at all times and what He was saying.) I thought to myself, *This is it. He's going to deal with this!* Then to my amazement, He asked me a question. "Where's your faith?"

I was surprised! For when He asked it, there was great displeasure in His voice – I knew I was being rebuked.

Then He continued, "When they turn the service over to you, call those forward who need healing, and I will heal them as a sign to you that I have spoken to you."

I thought to myself, *Heal them? I'M the one who needs help. What about me?* But He never said anything further to me about my situation.

Within a few minutes, the service was turned over to me. I did as Jesus instructed and called for those who needed healing and laid hands on them.

Afterwards, I was still puzzled as to why I was the one who got rebuked, for I was the one who was being attacked. It wasn't until later that I fully understood why Jesus rebuked me by asking, "Where's your faith?" I had become occupied with the enemy's threats, turning them over and over in my mind. Without realizing it, I had believed the suggestions the enemy had repeatedly fired against my mind; if I hadn't believed them, they wouldn't have unsettled and troubled me, no matter how many times he spoke them to my mind. I had become occupied with what I felt and heard instead of being occupied with what the Word said. I had listened to wrong thoughts and hadn't resisted them as I should; I had turned them over in my mind. Those fiery darts came against my mind to hold me in the mental arena and out of the spirit, which is the arena of faith.

If the enemy can hold you in the mental arena, he'll whip you. But if you'll hold him in the arena of faith by holding fast to your confession of the Word and refusing to entertain wrong thoughts, you'll whip him.

Satan is the god of this world (2 Cor. 4:4); he can make himself felt and heard in the natural and mental realm. But that's why we must hold him in the arena of faith, the spirit arena, instead of allowing him to hold us in the natural and mental arena.

It's so easy to slip back into the natural; that's the natural thing to do. When the enemy attacks, the opposition can be felt upon the mind and body, and it's so easy to become occupied with what we see and what we feel. But that's when we must hold to our faith in God's Word so that we aren't moved by what we feel and see, but instead, we walk by what we believe.

The devil may cause you to see, feel, and hear something, but he can't make you believe something. Refuse to let the pressure of what you may be seeing, feeling, and hearing change what you believe. Stand firm on God's Word. Hold fast to what His Word says.

Where Is What You Believe?

When Jesus asked me, "Where's your faith?" He was asking me, "Where is what you believe?" Without realizing it, I had set aside what I believed, for I had become occupied with the suggestions of the enemy. That's why Jesus rebuked me that day. I had not held fast to what I believed. I believed the right thing before the test came; I should have continued to believe the right thing in the face of the test. If I had believed the right thing during the test, I would have spoken what I believed and refused to think on the wrong thoughts.

Faith means you refuse to change what you believe just because you can see, feel, and hear the test. You believed the Word before the test – keep believing the Word in the face of the test. The reason the test comes is to try to get you to change what you believe. But hold fast to God's Word by speaking it and by thinking faith thoughts, which are the thoughts of the Word.

Can't Out-Think Wrong Thoughts

God said something to me years ago that I've stayed mindful of. "If you listen to everything the devil tells you, he'll steal from you everything I've ever blessed you with." You can start listening to and entertaining wrong thoughts without realizing it; that's why you have to pay attention to what you're allowing in your thought life.

Yes, you will hear the suggestions and the threats of the enemy, but you don't have to *listen* to them. You don't have to allow them to run free in your thought life; refuse to touch them in your thought life.

You can't overcome thoughts with thoughts; you overcome thoughts with words! You can't out-think wrong thoughts; you have to answer them with the Word of God.

Many endeavor to resist the devil by telling him to go, but then they pause a moment to see if it worked – to see if he left. They check their mind to see whether or not the thought is still there. Don't check your mind to see if it worked – that's not faith. When you resist the devil, answer him with the Word and then refuse to touch the wrong thought in your thought life; don't think about it – quit handling it mentally – let it go – let it go out of your thought life.

One strategy of the enemy is to suggest something repeatedly to the mind in hopes of getting you to believe it. Just because he suggests something repeatedly doesn't make it true. Repetition doesn't make it true. Answer those thoughts with the Word, no matter how many times he suggests them, and then start praising God for His Word. Praise holds you in the faith arena, the spirit arena, and out of the mental arena. Praise helps hold your thoughts on God and off opposing thoughts.

Don't Give Place to the Devil

Smith Wigglesworth tells of the time he was awakened one night when he felt an evil presence in his room. He rolled over to see Satan sitting on his bed. When Smith

Wigglesworth saw him, he said, "Oh, it's just you!" Then he rolled back over and went to sleep. That's faith! He wasn't awed by the enemy's presence. Yes, he felt his evil presence, but he didn't let what he felt occupy his attention or trouble him – he just went back to sleep. That's dominion! That's knowing who you are in Christ and walking in it!

Many times, when the enemy suggests thoughts to someone, instead of resisting them, they entertain them. They turn them over and over in their mind, and then the enemy keeps supplying them with more wrong thoughts because they opened the door to him by listening to the thoughts he suggested.

Genesis 3 gives the account of when Satan talked to Eve in the Garden of Eden. Instead of running him out of the garden (for they had the authority), Eve listened to him – she believed him and acted in line with what he said, and humanity has been affected ever since. Don't listen to wrong thoughts. Instead, resist them by answering them with the Word of God!

Ephesians 4:27 warns us, *"Neither give place to the devil."* The devil can't *take* a place in us, but we can give him a place. But if we can give him a place, we can also take back the place we gave him.

One way a Christian can open the door and give place to the devil is by listening to him, but they can close the door to him and take back the place from him by quit listening to him.

You need to think faith thoughts and speak faith words in your daily life so you don't give the devil a place in you.

Faith in the Face of the Storm

Jesus walked on the platform that day in the service and rebuked me by asking, "Where's your faith?" Jesus asked His disciples that same question. Luke 8:22-25 tells of the incident when Jesus was in the back of the boat sleeping when a great storm arose. The boat started filling up with water, and the disciples thought they would sink. Some of these men were fishermen; they were used to navigating through difficult conditions on the water, but the storm was great, and they became fearful.

Before they started their journey, Jesus had said, *"Let us go over unto the other side...,"* and they all believed they were going to reach the other side, so they launched off. But when the storm arose, they changed what they believed. They didn't believe they were going to reach the other side anymore – they believed they were going to sink.

They were feeling the boisterous wind. They were feeling the great bucking of the waves. They were seeing and feeling the water rise in the boat, but Jesus slept on. They were so overwhelmed with what they were feeling that they woke Jesus up so He could feel what they were feeling.

When Jesus awoke, He felt what the disciples felt, but He was undisturbed by it. He didn't allow what He felt to unsettle Him or change what He believed. He rebuked the wind and the raging of the water, then turned to the disciples and rebuked them by asking, "Where's your faith?" They weren't the ones who sent the storm. They weren't the ones who filled the boat with water. But they were the ones who changed what they believed because of what they felt.

In the face of the storm, Jesus exercised His authority. That's what we must do when we're faced with storms and opposition.

You're Authorized

Since Jesus is now seated at the right hand of the Father and we have been raised with Him, we're seated far above the devil and all evil spirits; we have authority over them. Our authority stems from that raised position. Since we have the authority to tread on serpents and scorpions and over all the power of the enemy without being hurt, then we are the ones who will have to exercise faith for ourselves in the face of any storm we encounter. He can't do it for us. God can't do for us what He has authorized and empowered us to do. *We* must hold to His Word. *We* must resist the devil. *We* must speak to the storms that arise in life. He handed the authority over circumstances to us, and we are the ones who must exercise that authority.

When Jesus walked on the platform that day and spoke to me, I was expecting Him to do something about my storm, but He didn't. He expected me to violate all that I was hearing and feeling and exercise my authority and not believe the threats of the enemy.

Don't wait for God to do something regarding a situation that may be troubling or unsettling you. *You* do something about it – you're authorized! Exercise your authority over the devil. Tell him to desist in his maneuvers against you.

God did all He's going to do about the devil when He sent Jesus to defeat and strip him of his power and authority over you. Jesus restored to the Church the authority that Adam had turned over to the devil when he sinned and committed high treason against God. Jesus handed you the authority to rule and reign as a king in this life over the circumstances that try to rise up against you, so you are the one who is authorized to do something with any opposition that arises. God doesn't need to do anything more for you. In fact, God can't do for you what He authorized you to do. The authority that He gave you over the enemy is total and complete, and it is more than sufficient to overcome any opposition.

Stay in the Arena of Faith

You must not allow the storm and what you may be feeling to change what you believe. Just because you can feel the test doesn't mean that your faith isn't working or that your faith has failed. You're going to feel the test. It doesn't feel good to the body or the mind; that's why you don't walk by what you see, feel, or hear, but you walk by faith. You don't lean to your head, but you lean to your heart, for that's where faith resides.

Jesus felt the storm that day in the boat, but He wasn't disturbed by it. He didn't let the storm change what He believed – but the disciples did, and that's why He rebuked them. Faith isn't moved by what it sees, hears, or feels – it's moved only by what it believes.

My spiritual father told the story of the time he was faced with a test and how the enemy tried to get him to become occupied with what he was feeling. "Check your body – it's shaking in fear," the enemy said. But he replied, "My body may be shaking, but that's not the real me. The real me is my spirit, and my spirit's not shaking!" With that, the enemy left, for my spiritual father refused to be occupied with the natural. He stayed in the arena of faith and overcame the threats of the enemy.

Yes, the body and the mind may feel the test, but your spirit is the real you. In your spirit is faith, and when you release your faith by speaking words of faith, you put the devil on the run.

The Two Houses

MATTHEW 7:24-27
24 Therefore whosoever heareth these sayings of mine, and doeth them, I will liken him unto a wise man, which built his house upon a rock:
25 And the rain descended, and the floods came, and the winds blew, and beat upon that house; and it fell not: for it was founded upon a rock.
26 And every one that heareth these sayings of mine, and doeth them not, shall be likened unto a foolish man, which built his house upon the sand:

27 And the rain descended, and the floods came, and the winds blew, and beat upon that house; and it fell: and great was the fall of it.

The house represents a man's life. The life that is built upon the rock is the man who is a doer of the Word of God. The life that is built upon the sand is the man who heard the Word, but failed to do it.

Notice that both houses encountered the storm – the rains descended, the floods came, and the winds blew and beat upon both houses. Both houses felt the storm, but one house stood while the other one fell.

Many years ago, as a young Christian, I faced a particular test that lasted a period of time. Because I was continuing to feel the storm, I wrongly thought that meant I was failing the test and that my faith wasn't working. After some time, I said to the Lord, "Lord, I feel like I have been beat on!" Then the Lord said to me, "That only means that you're in the last stage of the test." And He took me to this passage of scripture and showed me that a test can have 4 stages:

1. The rains descended – the house felt the storm in this first stage.

2. The floods came – what was left untouched by the rains was now engulfed in flood waters that had risen. In a flood, that which isn't anchored down will float away.

3. The winds blew – they can be felt and sometimes heard.

4. Beat upon that house – this implies blow after blow.

Up until this time, I had thought that if my faith was working, I wouldn't be feeling and hearing all that I was feeling and hearing and that the test wouldn't be continuing; I thought I was failing the test.

But that day, God corrected me. He asked me the question, "What determined whether or not the house passed the test?"

I answered, "Whether or not the house was still standing."

Then God asked me, "Are you still standing?"

Then I saw it! I answered, "Yes, I'm still standing! I'm still believing and speaking Your Word! I'm still walking with You."

The house passed the test because it was still standing at the end of the storm. I realized that the house had felt the storm. Even though the storm continued for a time, that didn't mean the house was failing. Likewise, my faith wasn't failing just because I felt the storm, and it wasn't failing just because the storm continued for a time. As long as I'm still standing on the Word at the end of the storm, I pass the test.

Being in faith doesn't mean you won't feel the storm or that the storm won't continue for a time, but it means that you refuse to change what you believe in spite of the storm you feel; regardless of how long the test may last, you just keep standing on the Word. That's faith!

That day was a turning point for me. I changed my focus away from the test I was feeling and occupied myself with the Word that I believed. Wrong thinking had held me in that test longer than I should have been in it, but when I got my thinking straightened out and started thinking in line with the Word, things started changing.

The Ringing Bell

In some old movies, there would sometimes be a scene of a church steeple that housed a bell. When an emergency would arise in the town, someone would go to the bell tower and hang on the rope to ring the bell, and then the townspeople would come running. After the bell had rung for a while, the person on the rope would jump off, yet the bell would continue to ring for a time, but then it would gradually slow down and finally grow quiet. The momentum kept the bell ringing for a time, even after the person had let go of the rope.

It seems that some tests can be similar. When a test arises, it may gain momentum, but when you exercise your authority over that situation, know that the devil flees – he's off the rope. Oh yes, the bell may continue to ring for a time, the test may seem to have continued movement for a time, but that's just from the momentum of the devil having been there. You just continue to stand your ground on God's Word, and know that the enemy has fled. If you do, the momentum of that test will decrease and decline until it finally ceases altogether.

When opposition arises, don't be occupied with what you may see, feel, and hear. Your authority works! The enemy is defeated; he has been reduced to nothing. You are seated *far above,* not just barely above, but *far above* all your enemies. The enemy is under your feet, and you are seated with Christ in heavenly places in the victory seat. Your authority over the enemy stems from that heavenly position you occupy – it is the victory seat. Exercise your authority and learn to laugh in the face of all opposition, regardless of what you may see or feel. You can laugh at the enemy and at circumstances, for you know the victory is yours.

Quench Fiery Darts

Renewing your mind with the Word of God will replace wrong thinking with right thinking. When you think right, you'll believe right. And when you believe right and speak right, you'll receive that which is right.

But you need to realize that every thought that comes to you doesn't always originate with you. As I stated earlier, the devil will seek to inject wrong thoughts into your thought life. When that happens, recognize that the thought is not your own and it must be resisted. Stop where you're at and say, "That's not my thought! Satan, I resist you in Jesus' Name, and you flee from me!" Then don't touch that thought again in your thought life; don't think about it.

The enemy will launch a fiery dart at your mind, but as you resist it by speaking the Word, the water of the Word will quench and put out that fiery dart (Eph. 6:16). Quench that fiery dart so that it can't spread and move to other arenas of your life. Fiery darts can strike with great force against the mind, but the water of the Word will quench it immediately. Speak your faith in God's Word, and refuse to be disturbed by any strategy of the enemy against you.

God Will Turn It Around

When God deals with us, He deals with us in line with His Word. When God speaks to you, it comes up from your spirit within and enlightens your mind. When the enemy speaks, it comes from the outside, against the mind. Learn to discern the difference.

Any thought that discourages us, puts us down, accuses us, points to our faults and failures, or tries to make us worry, fear, or doubt is from the enemy, and it is to be resisted.

God never deals with us along any of those lines. Even if we do miss God, that's not how He deals with us. God deals with us through His Word. God doesn't deal with us or correct us by sending tests and trials. Although we may learn from a test, that wasn't God's way of teaching us; He teaches us and deals with us through His Word.

Many times, Christians get the idea that if they missed God, then they have to accept defeat, but they don't. Victory isn't ours because we've done everything right, but victory is ours because *Jesus* did everything right. When we miss

God, we are to repent. When we repent, God forgives us and cleanses us from all unrighteousness – it is as though we never sinned – and then our faith will work. As we stand in faith, God will turn that situation around for us, for victory belongs to us.

Judge Experiences in Line With the Word

Don't believe that everything you hear is God speaking to you. Judge what you may hear by the Word of God. It doesn't matter if you hear an audible voice, have a dream, see a vision, see an angel, or have some other kind of experience; if it isn't in line with the Word, it's not from God. Any of those experiences that don't fully line up with the Word of God and don't minister peace to you are to be rejected. The devil can make himself felt in the natural arena, for he's the god of this world (2 Cor. 4:4). He can cause some supernatural manifestations in an attempt to deceive you, so don't receive every experience you may have. If it's not in line with the Word, reject it and refuse to touch it again in your thought life.

The Word doesn't instruct us to seek or pray for supernatural experiences like seeing visions, having dreams, or hearing an audible voice. By praying for them, you get off the Word, and then the devil may accommodate you, and it can make you unsound. These things happen only as God wills.

The Work of God

John 6:28 & 29 records a question the disciples asked Jesus, *"...What shall we do, that we might work the works of God? Jesus answered and said unto them, This is the WORK of God, that ye BELIEVE...."* To believe God is work – it's not play.

It's work to renew your mind with the Word of God. It's work to discipline your thought life. It's work to pay attention to the words that come out of your mouth. It's work to refuse to worry when circumstances are pressing on your mind and on your body. It's work to develop your spirit and to develop your faith so you can move forward with God. But what a grand, wonderful work it is!

What a joy to believe God and to work with Him! It's a glorious thing to get to stand on God's Word, for it never fails. It's a wonderful thing to get to lay the hand of faith to all that God has provided and draw it into every arena of life.

Keep feeding on the Word of God, for it will feed your spirit, renew your mind, and cause your faith to be robust. As one minister often said, "Feed your faith and starve your doubts!"

Chapter 5

Free From Worry

Several years ago, I was in a miracle service where my husband was teaching on divine healing. At the end of his sermon, he turned to me and asked me if I had anything from the Lord. I got up, took the microphone, and began speaking in other tongues; then I interpreted into English what I had spoken in other tongues. This happened three times.

What the Spirit said to us that night was that there are three primary ways sickness or defeat enters the life of the believer. These aren't the only ways, but they are three primary ways the Spirit gave. They are:

1. Through loss of peace

2. Through turning away from God's plan – In John 4:34, Jesus declared, *"...My meat is to do the will of him that sent me, and to finish his work."* Jesus was saying that just as meat nourished and sustained His body, doing the will of God nourished and sustained His life.

3. Through lack of gratitude – In Deuteronomy we're warned,

> **DEUTERONOMY 28:47-48 (AMPC)**
> 47 Because you did not serve the Lord your God with joyfulness of [mind and] heart [in gratitude] for the abundance of all [with which He had blessed you],
> 48 Therefore you shall serve your enemies....

Hebrews instructs us,

> **HEBREWS 13:15 (AMPC)**
> Through Him, therefore, let us CONSTANTLY AND AT ALL TIMES offer up to God a sacrifice of praise, which is the fruit of lips that thankfully acknowledge and confess and glorify His name.

As we praise God in gratitude for all of His blessings, it helps us to stay mindful of them, and they will continue to flow in our lives.

I want to focus on the first way the Spirit listed of how we open the door to sickness or defeat – through the loss of peace. That night the Spirit directed us to a passage recorded in Mark.

> **MARK 5:25-34**
> 25 And a certain woman, which had an issue of blood twelve years,
> 26 And had suffered many things of many physicians, and had spent all that she had, and was nothing bettered, but rather grew worse,
> 27 When she had heard of Jesus, came in the press behind, and touched his garment.
> 28 For she said, If I may touch but his clothes, I shall be whole.

> 29 And straightway the fountain of her blood was dried up; and she felt in her body that she was healed of that plague.
> 30 And Jesus, immediately knowing in himself that virtue had gone out of him, turned him about in the press, and said, Who touched my clothes?
> 31 And his disciples said unto him, Thou seest the multitude thronging thee, and sayest thou, Who touched me?
> 32 And he looked round about to see her that had done this thing.
> 33 But the woman fearing and trembling, knowing what was done in her, came and fell down before him, and told him all the truth.
> 34 And he said unto her, Daughter, thy faith hath made thee whole; go in peace, and be whole of thy plague.

Jesus told the woman, *"....Daughter, thy faith hath made thee whole; GO IN PEACE, AND BE WHOLE of thy plague."* The Amplified Classic Bible reads, *"...GO IN (INTO) PEACE AND BE CONTINUALLY HEALED and freed from your [distressing bodily] disease."* We see in this scripture the connection between peace and healing. If she would have lost her peace, she would have lost her healing.

In the service that night, God said to us that there are 3 primary ways people lose their peace:

1. Worry
2. Fear
3. Doubt and unbelief

Worry, panic, anxiety, doubt – all these are symptoms of fear. You must protect your peace from these things, for the loss of peace is an open door to the enemy.

Years ago, I was in the home of a world-renowned evangelist. As he was showing us through his home, I remarked how wonderful his backyard was; it was a lush garden with beautiful flowers and trees everywhere. When I commented on its beauty, he said, "Pay whatever it costs to buy peace." His comment has stayed with me through the years, for I have come to know how precious peace is. Nothing can take its place, and nothing else can substitute for the lack of it.

This evangelist had put forth effort and cost to create a beautiful garden that produced a peaceful atmosphere – it was worth the price. Jesus already paid the price for us to have peace, but we must put forth the effort to renew our minds with God's Word so that we can walk in and enjoy the peace He provided for us. To live a life of peace is worth the effort of renewing our minds.

No man can ever know true peace without Jesus, for He is the Prince of Peace. At His birth, the angels declared to the shepherds in the field, *"...on earth PEACE, good will toward men"* (Luke 2:14). His entrance into the earth was the entrance of peace. During Jesus' earthly ministry, peace is what governed Him, even in the face of violent opposition. In the face of every opponent and circumstance, none pulled Him out of peace.

What did peace look like in Jesus' life? It was the peaceful sleep in a boat that threatened to sink. It was the calm walk through a hostile crowd that threatened to push Him off a cliff in His hometown of Nazareth. It was the peaceful walk He took on the stormy waves of the sea. It was the peaceful stand He took when surrounded by the unbelieving. His faith in God held Him in peace and changed the complexion of every pressing circumstance and situation He faced.

What will peace mean in your life? Peace means that sleep and rest are possible when faced with seemingly impossible situations. Peace won't fall apart when faced with difficult circumstances. Peace doesn't mean the absence of difficulties, but rather peace means that you're resting on the Word and refusing to be disturbed in the face of difficulties. Peace won't resort to worry, fear, and doubt when pressed upon by challenges, for peace is a companion of faith. Peace considers the Word of God, not surrounding circumstances.

Your Measure of Faith

Romans 15:13 reads, *"Now the God of hope fill you with all JOY and PEACE in BELIEVING...."* Joy, peace, and faith are companions. When you're in faith, there's joy and peace in your heart, even though there may be opposition against the mind. You can measure your faith level by measuring your level of joy and peace. Your peace and joy level will equal your faith level.

Never go beyond your measure of faith. When you're beyond your measure of faith, you won't have joy or peace.

But when you're within your measure of faith, you will have joy and peace. To have success in your faith life, stay within your measure of faith. If you get out beyond your measure of faith, you will struggle and possibly fail. It's not doubt or unbelief to back up to get within your measure of faith, for when you're within your measure of faith, you'll succeed.

There may be times you have peace in your heart regarding a situation, but have opposition coming against the mind. Follow the peace in your heart regardless of any mental opposition you may have. You're always safe in following the peace in your heart, for that's one way God leads you.

Isaiah 55:12 reads, *"For ye shall go out with JOY, and BE LED FORTH WITH PEACE...."* Colossians 3:15 tells us, *"And let the peace of God rule in your hearts...."* The Amplified Classic Bible reads, *"And let the peace...from Christ rule (act as umpire continually) in your hearts [deciding and settling with finality all questions that arise in your minds...."* What does the umpire in a game do? He makes the call. When faced with a decision, let peace make the call.

One way God will lead you is through peace. Peace always accompanies the leading of God. If you have peace in your heart about doing something, follow it. If you don't have peace, then don't do it. If you do have peace in your heart about something, then you also have faith for it, for peace and faith are companions – they move together.

No More Worry

In the miracle service that night, the Spirit of God told us that one way we can open the door to sickness or defeat is through the loss of peace. And one of the ways that we can lose our peace is through worry.

The temptation to worry comes to all of us, but what does the Word instruct us to do when we're tempted to worry? Philippians 4:6 tells us, *"Be careful for nothing...."* The Amplified Classic Bible of this verse reads, *"Do not fret or have any anxiety about ANYTHING...."*

Someone may argue, "But you don't understand. I'm facing some difficulties and problems because of bad decisions *I've* made; I've brought this upon myself." It doesn't matter. You're not to fret or have any anxiety about *anything!*

Another person may argue, "Well, I'm in this bad situation because of what someone else did." It doesn't matter. You're not to fret or have any anxiety about *anything.* You're not to worry about *anything!* When the Word says "anything" it means *anything!*

How do you know if you're worrying? If you're thinking about it! Worry is meditation in the negative direction.

Worry opens the door to the enemy. Worry can break down the mind and the body if it is persisted in. God wants to spare us from the difficulties worry brings, so He tells us not to do it. When we obey God's Word and refuse to worry, then we'll be blessed. But anytime we disobey God's Word, it's a sin, so worry is a sin because God said not to do it.

If we're not to worry, then what are we to do? First Peter 5:7 tells us, *"Casting all your care upon him; for he careth for you."* The Amplified Classic Bible reads,

> **1 PETER 5:7 (AMPC)**
> **Casting the whole of your care [all your anxieties, all your worries, all your concerns, once and for all] on Him, for He cares for you affectionately and cares about you watchfully.**

He's watching. He sees you. He sees what you're facing, and He wants to take care of that problem, but He can't if you're going to hold onto it. Let it go! Tell the Lord that you're casting all your cares, worries, and anxieties on Him, and then let it go. Let it go from your thought life. Let it go from your conversations. Let it go!

When you cast your care on the Lord, you're putting the problem in His hands, and He can work on it. But if you take it back through worry, then He can't work on it because you've got it, not Him. Leave it in His hands – He can take care of it.

If the temptation to worry comes back to you, say, "No, I've cast that care over on the Lord, and I'm not taking it back. I've put it in His hands, and He's taking care of it."

If you're awakened in the middle of the night and tempted to worry, say, "I refuse to worry. I've cast that care over on the Lord, and I'm not taking it back. I've put it in His hands, and He's taking care of it." Then refuse to touch it in your thought life, refuse to think about it, and praise your way back to sleep.

Prayers that Work

Philippians 4:6 reads, *"Be careful for nothing; but in everything by prayer and supplication with thanksgiving let your requests be made known unto God."* The Amplified Classic Bible states, *"Do not fret or have any anxiety about anything...."*

Before you pray, you're going to have to quit fretting and quit being anxious; only then can you pray effectively. That's why the prayers of some people don't work, because they're worrying and fretting. You can't worry and be in faith at the same time. If prayer is to work, you must release faith, but worry will keep your faith from working.

It may not always be the easiest thing in the world to quit worrying about a situation, but we can quit worrying or God wouldn't have told us in His Word not to do it. God doesn't tell us to do something we can't do; He would be unjust in telling us to do something if it was impossible for us to do.

Before we ever pray, we need to deal with worry, then our faith will work and our prayers will work.

Take No Thought

MATTHEW 6:25-34

25 Therefore I say unto you, Take no thought for your life, what ye shall eat, or what ye shall drink; nor yet for your body, what ye shall put on. Is not the life more than meat, and the body than raiment?

26 Behold the fowls of the air: for they sow not, neither do they reap, nor gather into barns; yet your heavenly Father feedeth them. Are ye not much better than they?

27 Which of you by taking thought can add one cubit unto his stature?

28 And why take ye thought for raiment? Consider the lilies of the field, how they grow; they toil not, neither do they spin:

29 And yet I say unto you, That even Solomon in all his glory was not arrayed like one of these.

30 Wherefore, if God so clothe the grass of the field, which to day is, and to morrow is cast into the oven, shall he not much more clothe you, O ye of little faith?

31 Therefore take no thought, saying, What shall we eat? or, What shall we drink? or, Wherewithal shall we be clothed?

32 (For after all these things do the Gentiles seek:) for your heavenly Father knoweth that ye have need of all these things.

33 But seek ye first the kingdom of God, and his righteousness; and all these things shall be added unto you.

34 Take therefore no thought for the morrow: for the morrow shall take thought for the things of itself. Sufficient unto the day is the evil thereof.

Jesus is telling us not to worry about the daily necessities of food or clothing. If God doesn't want us to worry about the smallest details of the daily necessities of life, how much more He doesn't want us to worry about life's bigger needs.

In verse 27 the question is asked, *"Which of you by taking thought can add...."* To "take thought" is to worry. Things aren't added to your life through worry. Worry only subtracts – it never adds anything to your life.

Verse 31 reads, *"Therefore take no thought, saying...."* How do you take thoughts of worry? Through saying. Don't say thoughts of worry to others or to yourself.

Verse 31 continues to read, *"Therefore take no thought, saying, What shall we eat? or, What shall we drink? or, Wherewithal shall we be clothed?"* Notice that three questions are asked in this verse. This verse is warning us not to get into worry by asking a lot of questions: Why is this happening? What are we going to do? Where's the money going to come from?

Asking a lot of questions and trying to figure things out just holds you in the mental arena. You are to live in the arena of faith, the spirit arena. Faith in your heart will work even when you have questions or doubts in your mind; just lean to your heart and not to your mind. Don't try to figure everything out, but trust God to supply your needs. Release the faith that's in your heart by boldly confessing that God supplies all your needs (Phil. 4:19).

If you become occupied with the unknown things of life, you can get into worry. That's what faith is for – to deal with the unknown in life. We face the unknown with faith, not worry. We live by faith. We live our lives trusting God to lead, guide, and supply in the face of all that is unknown. Worry and doubt focus on questions, but faith trusts God in the face of the unknown.

Don't be occupied with what you don't know; rather, be occupied with the Word. Just walk in the light of what you do know; be a doer of the Word. If you need to know something more, trust God to bring you into the knowledge of it.

Moving Into the Unknown

Abraham was called by God to leave his family and home and to move into the unknown. He spent the rest of his days following God into the unknown because he was living and moving in faith. He left his home for a city whose Builder and Maker was God. God didn't give him a map; he just followed God into the unknown every day.

> **HEBREWS 11:8 (AMPC)**
> [Urged on] by faith Abraham, when he was called, obeyed and went forth to a place which he was destined to receive as an inheritance; and he went, although HE DID NOT KNOW OR TROUBLE HIS MIND ABOUT WHERE HE WAS TO GO.

Do you have the faith to move forward into the unknown? When God leads in a certain direction, faith will go, even when it doesn't know all the details; faith will go "not knowing," because faith isn't disturbed by all the "unknowns" of life, for it is focused on the One who knows all. We are to stay focused on the One who gives all the answers as we need them.

Questions are of the mental realm. Questions are of the natural realm. Answers are of the faith realm. Answers are of the spirit realm. Answers are of God's realm. There are no questions in God. There are no questions in God's realm. Instead of being occupied with the questions life presents, leave the natural realm and move into the faith realm. Trust the God of all answers to lead you through His Word and by His Spirit.

If you occupy yourself with the questions life offers instead of with God's Word, you will get into worry. Refuse to be occupied with or entertain thoughts of worry. Trust God to lead you into the answers you need. That is faith.

Faith doesn't mean the absence of questions, but faith means you refuse to be occupied with them. Faith refuses to worry about the unknown. Faith refuses to be captivated by the questions life presents. Refuse to linger back in the mire of questions that will bog you down and make your faith immobile. Move forward into the unknown, trusting the God who knows all. Faith trusts God.

Things Added to You

As we already read in the passage in Matthew 6:25-34, Jesus instructed us not to take thought for the things we have need of. We're not to worry about anything, for worry won't add anything to our lives.

Instead, He tells us to, *"...seek ye FIRST the kingdom of God, and his righteousness; and all these things shall be ADDED unto you"* (Matt. 6:33). As you seek first the Kingdom of God – putting spiritual things first, putting the Word first, and helping to further God's Kingdom in the earth – the things you need will be added to you. The things you need aren't *added* to you by seeking them through worry, but God is able to add to you as you seek first God's Kingdom and His righteousness.

Forget the Past

To live free from worry, discipline your mind not to touch in your thought life that which would trouble the mind. That would include troubling thoughts of the past; they must be forgotten. Once we confess any sin, 1 John 1:9 tells us that God is faithful and just to cleanse us of all unrighteousness by the Blood of Jesus. In the mind of God, that sin no longer exists. The past is dead and gone and should be forgotten. If you don't forget what should be forgotten, you'll open the door to the enemy because he'll keep bringing it back up to you and trip you up with it.

Paul stated, *"...but this one thing I do, FORGETTING those things which are behind, and reaching forth unto those things which are before"* (Phil. 3:13). You must forget what's behind you if you're to reach forward and lay hold of all that is in front of you.

You must not only forget your past, but you must also forgive and forget the past of others; forgive and forget the wrong that someone else may have done to you so that you can keep the door closed to the enemy.

Think on These Things

We are not to permit thoughts of worry in our thought life. In Philippians, Paul tells us what kind of thoughts we are to meditate on.

> **PHILIPPIANS 4:6-9**
> **6 Be careful for nothing; but in every thing by prayer and supplication with thanksgiving let your requests be made known unto God.**
> **7 And the peace of God, which passeth all understanding, shall keep your hearts and minds through Christ Jesus.**
> **8 Finally, brethren, whatsoever things are true, whatsoever things are honest, whatsoever things are just, whatsoever things are pure, whatsoever things are lovely, whatsoever things are of good report; if there be any virtue, and if there be any praise, think on these things.**
> **9 Those things, which ye have both learned, and received, and heard, and seen in me, do: and the God of peace shall be with you.**

The criteria a thought must meet before it is allowed into your thought life is listed above; it must be true, honest, just, pure, lovely, and of good report. Just because something may be true doesn't mean that it's pure or of good report; each thought must meet all the criteria and not just one of them. This is *all* part of living the life God planned for us – a life of faith and a life of peace, free from worry.

Chapter 6

Free From Fear

As I stated earlier, when you lose your peace, you open the door to the enemy. The three primary ways you lose your peace is through worry, fear, and doubt. In the previous chapter, I taught how to live free from worry, and in this chapter, we will see how to live free from fear.

Fear is not simply a feeling – fear is a spirit over which you have total authority and dominion. Second Timothy 1:7 reads, *"For God hath not given us the spirit of fear; but of power, and of love, and of a sound mind."* The Amplified Classic Bible of this verse reads,

> **2 TIMOTHY 1:7 (AMPC)**
> **For God did not give us a spirit of timidity (of cowardice, of craven and cringing and fawning fear), but [He has given us a spirit] of power and of love and of calm and well-balanced mind and discipline and self-control.**

God never deals with His people on the basis of fear. Any fear is not the dealing of God. Never entertain the thought that God is dealing with you or correcting you through fear. Fear is of the enemy; therefore, we have total authority over it.

It's important to recognize fear for what it is. Some have lived with fear for so long in different arenas of their life that they no longer recognize that the decisions they're making and the actions they're taking are in line with fear rather than faith.

Don't entertain thoughts of fear. Don't give place to the devil by listening to him. Yes, you may hear the threats that fear makes, but don't listen to them by turning them over in your mind. Each time thoughts of fear come, speak to them by saying, "Fear, I resist you. I refuse to take those thoughts. I will not be afraid. You leave me in Jesus' Name," and the devil will flee. But after you resist him, don't touch those thoughts of fear in your thought life; rather, begin praising God for His Word. That's how you hold your attention on God and off of troubling thoughts.

"For God hath not given us the spirit of fear; but of power, and of love, and of a sound mind" (2 Tim. 1:7). God has given us the spirit of power, love, and a sound mind.

Don't question your God-given power and authority over the spirit of fear; your authority over fear will work every time as you exercise it.

Don't allow fear to distort your understanding of how God deals with you. God deals with you based on love – not fear. God has no partnership with fear, so rebuke it.

As you renew your mind with the Word of God, you will enjoy a sound, disciplined, calm, and well-balanced mind. When the spirit of fear comes, don't allow it to unsettle your mind from off the Word; keep God's Word in your thoughts and in your mouth, and fear will be unsuccessful against you.

Violate Fear

If fear suggests something to you, violate it – don't act in line with it. Don't listen to it. Don't yield to it. Don't think about or believe what fear suggests. When you successfully resist fear in one arena, it may try to attack in another arena, but resist it and stand your ground.

Many, however, don't always recognize the movement of fear, so they don't always take a stand against it. One woman told me of a time when she was at work and was told by a co-worker that he was leaving the office early to go home because he was sick. When this woman heard that, she thought to herself, *I hope I don't get sick,* and she started rebuking sickness. But the next day, she got sick. When she related the story to me later, she said that she saw where she had missed it. It was fear that suggested to her that she might get sick. She believed what fear suggested and, in fear, started rebuking sickness. She opened the door to the devil by believing and acting in line with what fear suggested. Instead of rebuking sickness, she should have rebuked the spirit of fear.

We must recognize fear and resist it – not entertain it or act in line with it.

Dominion Over Anxiety and Panic

Anxiety and panic come from the spirit of fear. Speak to fear – tell it to leave you. You don't have to yield to anxiety and panic. Tell that fear to go in Jesus' Name, and it will obey you.

You may feel fear try to grip your mind and body, but that's just your flesh sensing the presence of the spirit of fear; that doesn't mean that fear is in your heart (your spirit). Your spirit is the real "you," and the real "you" isn't afraid; it doesn't matter that your flesh may sense it. Tell that spirit of fear to go, and it will.

Remember the story I told earlier of how the enemy tried to get my spiritual father to become occupied with what he was feeling. "Check your body – it's shaking in fear," the enemy said. But he replied, "My body may be shaking, but that's not the real me. The real me is my spirit, and my spirit's not shaking!" With that, the enemy left, for my spiritual father refused to be occupied with the natural. He stayed in the arena of faith and overcame the threats of the enemy.

Hold Fast to Your Victory

Colossians 1:13 tells us that God has delivered us from the power (the authority) of darkness and has translated us into the Kingdom of His dear Son. Satan has no authority over us. Fear has no authority over us. We're not a victim to it – we are in authority over it. However, for you to benefit from your authority, you must exercise it; exercise your authority over fear if it tries to oppose you.

If you have someone else pray for you when facing a test, you will still have to exercise faith in God's Word for yourself to *maintain* the victory you receive with the help of someone else's prayers and faith, for the enemy will always return to try to gain entrance again into your life. But hold fast to your victory in the face of any opposition and stand your ground against the enemy, refusing that which he tries to bring against you, and he will flee.

To live in victory, learn your authority in Christ and exercise it, for the enemy can't take advantage of those who know their authority, know who they are in Christ, and are exercising their authority.

To learn who you are "in Christ," take time to find the scriptures that contain "in Him, in Christ, in whom" and meditate on them, confessing them. That's how you build those truths in you so that you will benefit from being "in Christ."

You are redeemed from fear and from all the power of the enemy; the enemy has no authority over you. You are seated *far above* all your enemies. Remember that, speak that, and enjoy the benefits of that position!

Chapter 7

Keep Out Doubt

We must protect our peace so that we keep the door closed to the enemy. In the two previous chapters, I showed how we must protect our peace from worry and fear. In this chapter, we will see how we must protect our peace from doubt.

Romans 10:17 tells us, *"So then faith cometh by hearing, and hearing by the word of God."* Faith comes by hearing the Word of God. Faith doesn't come by praying for it, but faith comes as you gain knowledge of what God says in His Word. Great faith comes from great knowledge of God's Word. To have great faith, gain greater knowledge of His Word and act on it. Feeding on the Word of God, meditating on the Word (thinking deeply into it, muttering it to yourself, and talking to God about His Word), and acting on the Word will cause faith to grow strong.

God has given us His Word whereby strong faith can be obtained, but whether or not our faith is strong depends on us, not on God. The more we feed and act on His Word, making it part of our daily lives, the more our faith will grow. As our faith grows, doubt is run out.

Thoughts of doubt will come to everyone, but we're to refuse to let it in. When thoughts of doubt come, we're to resist them, saying, "Doubt, I resist you. I refuse to doubt!" James 4:7 tells us to, *"...Resist the devil, and he will flee from you."* When we resist doubt, we're resisting the devil, and he will flee.

Receive the Word

James wrote, *"...RECEIVE with meekness the engrafted word, which is able to save your souls* (or renew your mind)" (James 1:21). As we receive the Word into our minds and our spirits and allow that Word to dominate our thoughts and actions, then our minds will be renewed with God's Word and doubt will be run out.

We must agree with the Word if we're to benefit from it. Some hear what the Word says and reply, "Yes, I know what the Word says, BUT...." No, we can't argue against the Word and receive what it offers.

"But you don't understand my situation," someone may say. The Word that God has already given is enough for every situation; we don't need something different. We're not to reason against the Word, but receive it as our answer.

The Word is the answer in every situation. If we argue against the Word, we're arguing against our answer. We're not to argue against it – but agree with it. We're not to reason against it – but agree with it. Reasonings will lead us into questions and will feed doubt. We're not to reason against the

Word. We're not to analyze the Word – just do it! The Word doesn't need our mental analysis; it just needs our faith, our agreement, and our obedience. The spirit of man can receive and believe that which the mind can't always understand, so we're to receive the Word and act on it from our spirits.

To argue against the Word will hinder the process of renewing the mind. We're to agree with the Word from our hearts, receive it, and then act on it; it will bring great benefits.

Meekness

James tells us to, *"...receive with MEEKNESS the engrafted word..."* (James 1:21). Meekness, in this instance, doesn't refer to an outward behavior or in relation to other men, but meekness toward the Word. In W.E. Vine's *Expository Dictionary of New Testament Words,* one of the definitions of "meekness" is the accepting of God's dealings with us as good, and therefore we accept them without disputing or resisting.

A person who is meek toward the Word doesn't dispute with or resist God and His Word, but receives them; they receive the authority of the Word in their own life and recognize the authority of the Word over all opposition, circumstances, and situations.

In speaking of Moses, the Word says that he was the meekest man on the face of the earth (Num. 12:3). We can also see that Moses was greatly used by God. Those who are meek toward God and His Word are able to be used by God, for they don't dispute with or resist God's Word; they receive it and act on it. They are quick to submit to God's Word – they're quick to believe it – they're easily persuaded by the Word.

Abraham had the characteristic of meekness toward God and His Word because he was quick to believe; he didn't resist, argue against, reason against, or doubt what God had said.

> **ROMANS 4:20 & 21**
> **20 He** (Abraham) **staggered not at the promise of God through unbelief; but was STRONG IN FAITH, giving glory to God;**
> **21 And being FULLY PERSUADED that, what he** (God) **had promised, he was able also to perform.**

Abraham was strong in faith by giving glory to God and by being fully persuaded that God was able to do what He said. You, too, will be strong in faith by giving glory to God and by being fully persuaded that God is able to do what He said.

Abraham was fully persuaded. God didn't have to coerce him into believing Him. Abraham was quick to believe; he didn't stagger at the promise of God through unbelief – he didn't reason against or doubt God's Word. Oh yes, Abraham was human, just like the rest of us, but he didn't allow his mind to talk him out of what God said. He believed and held fast to God's Word.

Someone who is meek toward God and His Word is quick to believe the Word, and they're quick to believe teaching and preaching that's in line with God's Word; they aren't skeptical and critical of the Word. No, they're not gullible, willing to swallow anything offered them, but they're not hard to be convinced when it comes to God's Word. They come to God's Word ready to be persuaded by it.

We are to be quick to receive the Word. We're not to be quick to receive a testimony of doubt, thoughts of fear, thoughts of worry, condemning accusations, or an evil report; we are to be quick to resist those. But we're to be quick to receive and believe the Word. What God says is true. We honor God when we believe His Word and act on it.

The Engrafted Word

James tells us, *"... receive with meekness the ENGRAFTED word..."* (James 1:21). When anything is engrafted, it becomes a part of something. For the Word to become part of our lives and make a difference, it must become engrafted. It can only become engrafted as we feed on the Word of God; our minds, as well as our spirits, must be fed on God's Word.

Our minds are the gateway to our spirits; our minds allow the Word to flow or hinder the Word from flowing into our spirits. We're not to let the arguments, the reasonings, or the analysis of the mind to rise up and hinder or block the flow of the Word into our spirits. We are to accept God's Word.

For the Word to become engrafted, it has to reach beyond our intellects and sink into our spirits; this is done as we take time to meditate on the Word. We're to, *"...receive with meekness the ENGRAFTED word...."*

Exercising Faith Every Day

The just shall live by faith (Heb. 10:38). We are to live a life of faith. Faith must be expressed and exercised every day. The inward man is renewed day by day (2 Cor. 4:16). Every day we must feed and nourish our spirit man. Every day we must walk by faith. Every day we must think faith thoughts and speak faith words. Every day we must release and express our faith through faith words and faith actions. Every day we must exercise our authority over the enemy when he opposes us.

Every day we must renew our minds with the Word of God. Every day we must cast down imaginations and bring every wrong thought into captivity, refusing to let them loose in our thought life, thereby keeping the door closed to the enemy.

As we feed on God's Word and act on it, we will shut doubt out of our lives, and our faith will grow strong and robust, and our lives will bear much fruit.

Chapter 8

Freedom From Depression – The Praise Cure

If worry is persisted in, it can open the door to wrong things, including depression. But if you'll be a doer of the Word, regardless of what you may feel, you can exit out of depression and keep the door closed to it.

Every believer must renew their mind with the Word of God. This is done by feeding on the Word and by being a doer of the Word. To be a doer of the Word includes bringing your thought life in line with God's Word. Wrong thoughts come to everyone, but all thoughts that are not in line with His Word are to be rejected. Refuse to listen to or turn troubling thoughts over in your mind; refuse to think about them. Refuse to believe the wrong thing. Stand your ground on God's Word, answering those thoughts with the Word of God. Resist the devil, and he will flee (James 4:7).

Isaiah 61:3 speaks of, *"...the garment of praise for the spirit of heaviness...."* In the face of seeming heaviness and depression, instead of listening to or turning troubling thoughts over in your mind, put God's praises in your mouth.

Praising God from your heart plays a role in exiting out of heaviness and depression or any test.

One way you release your faith is through praising the Lord from your heart, and when your faith is flowing, God's power will meet your faith; when you release your faith, the power of the greater One within you will flow.

You're not praising God based on how you feel, but you're praising God based on who He is and for the great things He has done for you. You're not praising God because of the difficulty or the test, for He didn't send it, but you're praising God because His power, which belongs to you, is greater; His power will deliver you. You praise God in the face of adversity because of what you know – you know that Jesus already won the victory for you, so you praise Him for that.

Even if your praises seem dry and difficult at first, just keep praising, for as you do, you'll begin to move out of the natural and the mental arena and into the spirit; and when you start operating out of your spirit, things will start changing. When you release your faith in Him through praise, God's power starts changing things. Praising God brings the anointing, and the anointing destroys the yoke (Isa. 10:27).

The Praise Cure

Years ago, there was a time when I was faced with a difficult situation. I prayed, I fed on the Word, and I confessed the Word faithfully. But one day, the Spirit prompted me to spend most of my time praising the Lord, so I did. For the next week, I just praised the Lord continuously. If I was by myself, I would do it aloud. If I was around other people, I would do it quietly to myself. Regardless of what I felt, I kept at it. When it seemed dry, I just kept at it. As I did, I realized that I had moved from "trying" to trusting and resting. I hadn't realized that all the praying, studying, and confessing I had been doing previously was from a place of "trying" to get victory instead of trusting and resting in the victory that was mine already. I realized I had left faith and had slipped into the mental arena – trying to work for victory instead of resting in the victory Jesus had already gotten for me. (It's so easy to slip out of faith and back into the mental arena.) Spending much time praising God moved me out of the mental arena and back into the spirit and into faith; then when I started operating in faith, God's power began flowing and things started changing, and I got on the other side of that test.

When faced with a test, praising the Lord holds you in the spirit arena, which is the arena of faith, and out of the mental arena.

Now, the natural mind may reason that simply praising God isn't enough to deliver you from a difficult situation – but it is, for praise is one way you release your faith in the power of God, and the power of God can change your situation.

Praise – Your Exit and Your Entrance

Acts 16 tells of when Paul and Silas were beaten and thrown in prison. Locked up in chains, they prayed and sang praises. As they praised, a great earthquake came, and their chains fell off and the prison doors opened. It wasn't while they were praying that the answer showed up, but while they were praising. Some people need to stop praying about their situation and go to praising. It's right to pray, but don't stop there; start praising, for praise is the voice of faith.

As God's people marched around the walled city of Jericho, God directed them to lift their voices in shouts of praise. As they did, God's power was released. The walls came down, and they won a mighty victory. They could have reasoned that shouting praises doesn't make walls fall, but their obedience to praise released God's mighty power on their behalf, and the walls came down!

Praising played a role in Paul and Silas getting *out* of jail, and praising played a role in God's people getting *into* Jericho. In life, you sometimes need to come out of a place, and you sometimes need to get into a place – praising plays a role in you moving out or moving in.

Praise gets your focus off you and your circumstances, and puts your focus on God, the greater One. When you praise God from your heart, faith is released – and God goes where faith puts Him!

Apply the Praise Cure

One woman minister, who had a healing ministry, tells of the time a man was requesting prayer for his wife. She was sick at home with a contagious, life-threatening illness. When the man made the request for prayer for his wife, the woman minister said, "Let's apply the praise cure," and the two of them stood together and praised God for His mighty healing power on behalf of the man's wife. After a time of praising God together, the man went home to find his wife completely healed. There had been open sores broken out all over her body from the disease, but every one of them had completely dried up.

Praising God doesn't move Him, but it moves you into faith, and God answers faith. Praising God helps keep your focus and attention off the difficulty and onto the greater One.

It's right to pray, it's right to study, it's right to make confessions of the Word, but don't leave out the mighty flow of praise. As Psalm 34:1 says, *"I will bless the Lord at all times: his praise shall CONTINUALLY be in my mouth."*

As you daily praise the Lord, making it a lifestyle, you keep your faith flowing, and you will find that heaviness and depression will be a thing of the past.

The Joy of the Lord

Nehemiah 8:10 tells us, *"...the joy of the Lord is your strength."* Joy is a fruit of the born-again spirit; it is resident in the believer. One way that joy is released is through rejoicing. The joy of the Lord is your strength, so as you rejoice in God and His Word, you're strengthened to overcome opposition.

We're not to be joyful and praising God only when everything is going good and everything is in place. We're not to be joyful only when we feel like it, but we're to be joyful in the face of all opposition – no matter what it may be. That's when we experience the real value, benefits, and power of joy and praise. Joy is a spiritual force and a spiritual flow from within our spirits. When things are seemingly out of place and not as we wish them to be, we are to make the decision to stay in the flow of joy through rejoicing and praising the Lord.

To praise God and to be joyful are not simply feelings; rather, they are a decision – a choice we make. We are to be joyful and praise God because we know that no matter what the opposition may be, the greater One is in us; we are to rest and recline ourselves upon the greater One within. We are not to struggle to overcome a situation, but we are to trust Him to put us over, for we know that no opposition is equal to the greater One in us.

There's great power in joy, and when you open your mouth to praise God, you release the flow of that power. Praising God helps you to live mindful of the greater One within and helps you to keep your focus off of opposition and opposing circumstances; it helps you to take advantage of your victorious position in Christ, where you are seated far above difficulties, opposition, depression, and all your enemies.

Chapter 9

No Condemnation – Forget It!

> *There is therefore now no condemnation to them which are in Christ Jesus, who walk not after the flesh, but after the Spirit.*
>
> – Romans 8:1

"There is therefore NOW NO CONDEMNATION...." This verse shows us that God put a timeline to the end of condemnation – now! Condemnation is to come to an end in your life now! Condemnation will keep your faith from working, so you must put an end to condemnation in your life right now, refusing to let it in. God put an end to condemnation to those who are in Christ, and if you're born again, you're in Christ. God never deals with you along the lines of condemnation; He doesn't condemn you.

The word "condemned" means pronounced to be wrong, guilty, and worthless; sentenced to punishment or destruction. That is no description of the child of God, for Jesus took our place in punishment; He was condemned so we could be free.

For us to yield to a sense of condemnation is to forget what Jesus did for us. A sense of condemnation and guilt is not part of God's dealings with His children, and it is to be resisted. Those who yield to a sense of condemnation and guilt will find their faith weakened and unable to receive from God. It takes faith to receive from God, and there is no faith attached to condemnation; it can't conduct faith.

Those who yield to condemnation will not only find their faith inoperative, but condemnation can open the door to depression. We are not to give place to condemnation; we must resist its entrance into our lives. If the door has been opened to condemnation, then it can be closed by being a doer of the Word.

Forgive Yourself

Because we are so acquainted with our own faults, failures, and shortcomings, there is the temptation to yield to condemnation, but we must reject it.

We may have found it easier to forgive others who may have wronged us than to forgive ourselves when we miss God, but if our faith is to work, and if we are to keep the door closed to condemnation, we must forgive ourselves. Some live under worry, guilt, condemnation, fear, and depression simply because they haven't forgiven themselves.

MARK 11:23-25
23 For verily I say unto you, That whosoever shall say unto this mountain, Be thou removed,

> **and be thou cast into the sea; and shall not doubt in his heart, but shall believe that those things which he saith shall come to pass; he shall have whatsoever he saith.
> 24 Therefore I say unto you, What things soever ye desire, when ye pray, believe that ye receive them, and ye shall have them.
> 25 And when ye stand praying, FORGIVE, if ye have ought against any....**

Just as Mark 11:23 & 24 tells us how faith works, verse 25 tells us one of the primary things that will keep our faith from working – unforgiveness. *"And when ye stand praying, FORGIVE, if ye have ought against any..."* (Mark 11:25). Failing to forgive others will keep our faith from working, but failing to forgive ourselves when we've missed it will also keep our faith from working, and it will open the door to condemnation. If we're to be doers of the Word, we must forgive ourselves.

Forget It

First John 1:9 reads, *"If we confess our sins, he is faithful and just to forgive us our sins, and to cleanse us from all unrighteousness."* If you miss God and sin, stop right there and confess it to God and repent. When you miss it, confess it as quickly as you can, then you won't leave an open door for the enemy. If you will confess it, God is faithful and just to forgive you and to cleanse you from all unrighteousness.

When we sin, we lose our sense of righteousness. But when we confess our sins, He cleanses us from our unrighteousness, and our sense of righteousness – our sense of right standing with God – is restored to us.

When God forgives you, He forgets it – never to be remembered again. When you confess your sin, not only does God forgive and forget it, but you must forgive yourself and forget it, too.

To fail to forgive yourself is to doubt that God forgave you. When you act in faith on God's Word, you take Him at His Word – you believe that He forgives, cleanses, and forgets it when you confess it, and so you forgive yourself, too.

Now, the enemy, who is the accuser of the brethren, will accuse you and try to remind you of where you missed it, but you must answer him with the Word. "No you don't, devil. God has forgiven me and forgotten it, and I've forgiven myself and forgotten it, and I'm not taking that thought."

Forgiveness Is a Decision

Forgiveness isn't a feeling – it's a decision. You don't forgive others or yourself based on feeling, but by a decision. When bad feelings or memories try to come to you against someone you've forgiven, you must reject them. You are to say, "No, I've forgiven them, and I will not remember it anymore." You must not only do that when you've forgiven others, but also when you've forgiven yourself. When you do that, the past can't hold you. Don't allow yourself, or the enemy, to accuse you with your past.

First John 4:16 tells us, *"And we have known and BELIEVED THE LOVE that God hath to us...."* We can be so quick to believe the accusations of the enemy against us, but instead, we should be quick to believe the love God has toward us. We are not to believe the enemy who accuses, but believe God's love for us.

Forget, Reach Forth, and Press

When God forgives, He forgets. Our sins are worthy of one thing – forgetting! When God forgives you, He also cleanses you. It is as though you never missed it. What would you dare to do for God, or what could you believe God for, if you had never missed it? The blood of Jesus puts you in that very place – as though you never missed it.

If there's anyone who could have been held back by their past, it would have been the Apostle Paul. He consented to the murder of Christians and was on the road to Damascus to imprison more believers when he had his encounter with Jesus. But Paul didn't allow his past to keep him from moving forward with God and from fulfilling all God had for him, for he wrote to Timothy, *"I have fought a good fight, I have FINISHED my course, I have kept the faith"* (2 Tim. 4:7).

Paul, who went on to write half of the New Testament, tells us how he moved beyond his past to become one of the Church's finest leaders.

PHILIPPIANS 3:13 & 14
13 ...this one thing I do, FORGETTING those things which are behind, and REACHING FORTH unto those things which are before,
14 I PRESS toward the mark for the prize of the high calling of God in Christ Jesus.

Paul said he did three things: I forget, I reach forth, I press.

Forgetting the past is the first thing to be done before you can fully reach forth and press to what's ahead. Failure to forget holds you back. You'll not get past what you fail to forget. Failure to forget is an indication that you have yet to forgive yourself; and unforgiveness, toward others or yourself, is your stopping place. There's no movement forward without forgiveness and forgetting.

There's so much more in front of you than behind you. Forget the past so you can fully reach forth and lay hold of the greatness of God's plan that's ahead for you.

God Will Not Remember

ISAIAH 43:25 & 26
25 I, even I, am he that blotteth out thy transgressions for mine own sake, and will not remember thy sins.
26 Put me in remembrance: let us plead together: declare thou, that thou mayest be justified.

God tells us that He blots out our transgressions for *His* own sake. He blots them out, not only for *our* sake, but for

His sake. What does God mean by that? God wants to bless us, but sin keeps blessings away from us. God blots out our transgressions and forgets our sins so that we can receive God's blessings – all that He has provided for us.

God also blots out our transgressions and forgets our sins for His own sake so that we can be co-laborers with Him in the earth, carrying out His great work in the earth.

Verse 25 also tells us that God says, *"I...WILL NOT REMEMBER thy sins."* Not remembering our sins is a choice of God's will. He has set His own will to no longer remember our sins. We must also agree and comply with His will and choose to no longer remember our sins. When we truly repent, we can be assured of God's will to forgive us and forget our sins.

Boldness Before God

In the next verse, Isaiah 43:26, God tells us to, *"Put me (God) in remembrance: let us plead together: declare thou, that thou mayest be justified."* The Amplified Classic Bible reads, *"Put Me in remembrance [remind Me of your merits]; let us plead and argue together. Set forth your case, that you may be justified (proved right)."*

Isaiah 43:25 lets us know that when we confess our sins to God, our sins and transgressions are blotted out and forgotten. So when we come to verse 26, which deals with coming to God in prayer, sin isn't present anymore. Now we can come boldly before God with our requests, for we are clean.

When we come to God in prayer to lay our needs before Him, we are not to come with words of condemnation, guilt, and failures of the past in our mouths; rather, we are to come before Him knowing that He has blotted out and forgotten all confessed sins. We are to come to Him with faith in our mouths. We are to come to Him with His Word in our mouths, for that's when we'll receive. Our faith won't work with failures and sins of the past in our mouths. Guilt and condemnation are poor receivers; they will keep us from being bold to lay hold of and receive needed answers from God.

The enemy is the accuser of the brethren, and when you pray, he may try to remind you of your past in an attempt to keep you from receiving from God. But answer him with the Word, stating that you know your sins are blotted out and forgiven; then rise up in faith and lay hold of that which God has provided for you.

Live free and walk free from the past, failures, sin, guilt, and condemnation so that you can freely receive all God has made yours.

Great Is Thy Faith

MATTHEW 15:21-28
21 Then Jesus went thence, and departed into the coasts of Tyre and Sidon.

**22 And, behold, a woman of Canaan came out of the same coasts, and cried unto him, saying, Have mercy on me, O Lord, thou son of David; my daughter is grievously vexed with a devil.
23 But he answered her not a word. And his disciples came and besought him, saying, Send her away; for she crieth after us.
24 But he answered and said, I am not sent but unto the lost sheep of the house of Israel.
25 Then came she and worshipped him, saying, Lord, help me.
26 But he answered and said, It is not meet to take the children's bread, and to cast it to dogs.
27 And she said, Truth, Lord: yet the dogs eat of the crumbs which fall from their masters' table.
28 Then Jesus answered and said unto her, O woman, great is thy faith: be it unto thee even as thou wilt. And her daughter was made whole from that very hour.**

This Canaanite woman had no covenant with God – she wasn't a Jew. God's Word was not the standard by which she lived and conducted her life. But when she heard of Jesus, she was quick to believe that He could deliver her demon-possessed daughter. When she came to Jesus with her need, she didn't come to Him speaking of her godless lifestyle. She didn't come to Him thinking about and speaking of her sins, her past, or her failures. She didn't come to Him with reasons in her mouth of why she shouldn't or couldn't receive. When she came to Him, she had one thing in mind – receiving – receiving deliverance for her daughter. And Jesus called her a woman of great faith.

When faced with a need, we are to come to God expecting to receive! We are to come to God with His Word in our mouths. We are to come to God with faith in our mouths. We are to come to God knowing that His best belongs to us, and that when we confess our sins, Jesus' blood has washed away our past and has made us righteous – we are in right standing with God. All Christ has provided belongs to us! So we are to take it!

We are also to look to the help the Holy Spirit gives. If there is something we need to correct, adjust, or do, we are to look to Him to lead and direct us in that. He is our great Helper, and as we look to Him and follow how He leads us, He will lead us into receiving and into victory.

Great faith doesn't hold to the past, to failures, or to sin, but it holds to the Word. Because sin is blotted out and forgotten, great faith won't look behind to the past that is dead and gone, but it reaches forth to that which is before it, pressing past all hindrances and opposition. The past is dead and gone, and it is to be forgotten, for what's ahead is so much greater than that which is behind.

Chapter 10

The Other Side of the Test

Beloved, think it not strange concerning the fiery trial which is to try you, as though some strange thing happened unto you:

But REJOICE....

— 1 Peter 4:12 & 13

Beloved, do not be amazed and bewildered at the fiery ordeal which is taking place to test your quality, as though something strange (unusual and alien to you and your position) were befalling you.

But insofar as you are sharing Christ's sufferings, REJOICE....

— 1 Peter 4:12 & 13 (AMPC)

Any time you move forward in God, come into a new phase or room of ministry, come into greater revelation of the Word, or come into a deeper place of the Spirit, the enemy is going to oppose you to try to hinder or block your progress. Don't think it's strange that the fiery trial comes. Don't slip into the mental arena or become fearful, wondering why the enemy seeks to oppose you. He will contest you every inch of the way, but as you stand your ground on the Word of God, you will get safely to the other side of the test.

Peter tells us what to do in verse 13 to overcome this opposition – rejoice! Rejoice your way through it, for the One who is in you is greater than that which opposes you.

Always remember in the face of all opposition that the enemy is a defeated foe. Always remember that Jesus spoiled principalities and powers (Col. 2:15); He disarmed them, He exposed them as shattered, empty and defeated, and He reduced them to nothing. Jesus' defeat of the enemy is total and complete. You don't have to do anything else to defeat the devil – he is defeated! You don't have to fight him – he is a defeated foe already! Jesus did that for you! The only fight we're told to engage in is the good fight of faith (1 Tim. 6:12). You fight the good fight of faith by taking your stand on the Word of God and refusing to be swayed from it. This is done by speaking and holding to God's Word in the face of all opposition. Stand your ground rejoicing, for victory is yours, no matter what opposes you.

"...Greater is he that is in you, than he that is in the world" (1 John 4:4). The greater One is in you. The Spirit of God on the inside of you is the greater One, and the devil is the lesser one! The devil is no match for the greater One

that's in you. You don't have to hold out against the devil – he has to hold out against you!

Step Over It!

Paul stated, *"For a great door and effectual is opened unto me, and there are many adversaries"* (1 Cor. 16:9). Where are the adversaries? They are at the door trying to hinder or block your entrance into the new places God is leading you. But as you keep moving forward and refuse to draw back, you will move past all opposition. As Peter said, don't think this opposition is a strange thing – it is a strategy of the enemy to try to hinder or block your progress. Just keep moving ahead!

Jesus told us, *"Behold, I give unto you power* (authority) *to tread on serpents and scorpions, and over all the power of the enemy: and nothing shall by any means hurt you"* (Luke 10:19). One definition for the word "tread" is to step over. So we could read this verse as follows and still be correct, "Behold, I give you authority to *step over* serpents and scorpions, and over all the power of the enemy: and nothing shall by any means hurt you."

When opposition arises to try to hinder or block your progress, you are authorized to step over it and keep on going. Don't allow that opposition to stop your progress – keep moving ahead. Keep moving forward with God into the next place He's leading you. As you step over all opposition, *"...nothing shall by any means hurt you."* You have Jesus' Word on it!

Stir Up the Gift

Paul told Timothy,

II TIMOTHY 1:6 & 7
6 Wherefore I put thee in remembrance that thou STIR UP THE GIFT OF GOD, which is in thee by the putting on of my hands.
7 FOR GOD HATH NOT GIVEN US THE SPIRIT OF FEAR; but of power, and of love, and of a sound mind.

Paul was telling Timothy not to let fear keep him from moving with the gift of God that was in him, but to stir up the gift.

At a time of advancement and promotion or coming into new phases or rooms of ministry, fear may try to oppose you. But God has not given us the spirit of fear; we have authority over it, and we are to resist it. We are to stir up the gift of God within and boldly continue to move forward with God.

Stand Your Ground

All spiritual progress is going to be opposed. Every advancement and new phase or room of ministry is going to be opposed. That opposition includes attacks on the mind. The enemy will try to hold you out of the arena of faith, the spirit arena, and in the mental arena by launching fiery darts against the mind, but you are to quench every one of those fiery darts through faith in God's Word. Refuse to turn those wrong thoughts over in your mind. Instead, answer them by speaking God's Word from your spirit. When you successfully resist the devil in one arena, he may move to another arena, but stand your ground firmly on God's Word, for God's Word will never fail you as you hold fast to it.

When Jesus was advancing into His earthly ministry, He faced a season of testing and temptation that lasted 40 days and nights, but as He answered every temptation by speaking the Word of God, He emerged victorious and full of the Spirit (Luke 4). When faced with tests, we are to rejoice, for we know that as we stand our ground by speaking the Word of God, regardless of what we see, feel, or hear, we will reach the other side of the test, for the victory is ours!

Unfailing Faith

Before Jesus was arrested, He told Peter, *"...Satan hath desired to have you, that he may sift you as wheat: But I have prayed for thee, THAT THY FAITH FAIL NOT..."* (Luke 22:31 & 32). Jesus prayed that Peter's faith wouldn't fail. Jesus was letting Peter know that by holding to his faith in God's Word he would overcome the enemy's strategies against him.

The enemy would like to steal your faith, for it's with your faith that you conduct business with Heaven and receive all that God has provided. It is by faith in God that you move past all opposition and lay hold of all God has made yours. No matter what the opposition, hold fast to your faith in God's Word. Feed your faith on God's Word, think and speak faith words, act on God's Word, and rest and recline yourself on God's Word, for victory is yours.

Look Past the Test

"Looking unto Jesus the author and finisher of our faith; who for the joy that was set before him endured the cross..." (Heb. 12:2). We are to look to Jesus as our example when faced with opposition. When Jesus was faced with the Cross, He endured by focusing on *"the joy that was set before him"* – He focused on what was on the other side of the Cross. When faced with the Cross, He looked past it, clear through to the other side. He looked past the Cross to the joy of His resurrection, His ascension to the Throne, His eternal reign at the right hand of the Father, and bringing many sons to glory.

What must you do when faced with a test? The same thing Jesus did. Look past it! There's only one way to look past it – with the eye of faith. By faith, look past all opposition and see clear through to the other side; see what you will move into on the other side of the test.

Keep your eyes off the test, and put your focus on the joy that's waiting for you on the other side of it. The test is only trying to block from your view all that awaits you on the other side – greater anointing, greater revelation, a greater flow of ministry, and a greater walk with God.

Rejoice! There are great things on the other side of the test! Your greatest days are ahead of you, so meet them with faith!

Chapter 11

Count It All Joy

My brethren, count it all JOY when ye fall into divers temptations;

Knowing this, that the trying of your FAITH worketh patience.

– James 1:2 & 3

Consider it wholly JOYFUL, my brethren, whenever you are enveloped in or encounter trials of any sort or fall into various temptations.

Be assured and understand that the trial and proving of your FAITH bring out endurance and steadfastness and patience.

– James 1:2 & 3 (AMPC)

Why are we to count it all joy when faced with a trial or temptation? For it is another opportunity to stand on God's Word in faith and prove His faithfulness to fulfill His Word in our lives. How do we count it a joy to stand on God's Word? By rejoicing and praising God for His Word right in the face of the test and trial, for we know that God's Word cannot fail.

When you rejoice from your heart, you're releasing your faith in God, and God's power meets faith; God's power changes things.

Even if you're facing difficulties because of wrong decisions or wrong steps you've made, as you stay in faith and count it a joy to stand on God's Word, God will turn it around for you.

When God led His people out of Egypt, He led them through the wilderness on their way to the Promised Land. Their journey through the wilderness should have only lasted several days, but because they didn't walk by faith, they lingered in a place they should have only passed through – they lingered there for 40 years.

If we don't operate in faith, we could linger in a certain place or test we should only pass through. But by rejoicing in the face of difficulties, we hold ourselves in the flow of faith, and faith will cause us to pass through every test and trial victoriously. We're not rejoicing because we're going through a trial or temptation, but we're rejoicing because we know the victory is already ours as we stand on God's Word.

The Strength of Joy

Nehemiah 8:10 tells us, "...*the joy of the Lord is your strength*...." Joy is a fruit of the born-again spirit; it is resident in the believer. One way that joy is released is through rejoicing. The joy of the Lord is your strength, so as you rejoice in God and His Word, you're strengthened to overcome opposition.

Joy can be released through laughter, but faith can also be released through laughter. Faith will cause you to laugh at the devil and in the face of circumstances, for you know that Jesus has already defeated the enemy and given you the victory. Learn to release faith through laughter.

Paul's Instructions To Rejoice

In 2 Corinthians 11:23-27, we find the list of some of the tests that Paul endured, yet his faith continued to flourish, and he fulfilled his ministry in the full force of faith. How was he able to endure imprisonments, beatings, betrayals, stoning, and other hardships without wavering or compromise? We can see one answer to this in his letter to the Philippians. *"...REJOICE in the Lord"* (Phil. 3:1). *"...Delight yourselves in the Lord and CONTINUE TO REJOICE THAT YOU ARE IN HIM"* (AMPC). *"REJOICE in the Lord always: and again I say, REJOICE"* (Phil. 4:4). Paul wrote these instructions to rejoice from jail. He wrote to others reminding them that because they are in Christ, they have something to rejoice about, and that they should live rejoicing. These instructions give us a glimpse into Paul's life and a key to his success – he lived rejoicing, and as he rejoiced, he was strengthened in the face of great opposition.

Rejoicing holds your attention on God and His Word instead of on the difficulty and opposition; it holds you in the arena of faith.

We are to have a lifestyle of rejoicing in the Lord – rejoice always. To rejoice in the Lord is to rejoice that we are in Christ. We are to rejoice over what our union with Him means to our lives. That union means victory for every arena of life: spiritually, mentally, physically, and materially. All that is His is ours – that's something to rejoice about!

A Full Joy Level

When driving a vehicle, we have to refuel it so we don't run out of gas and get stranded alongside the road somewhere; we can't reach our destination on empty. Spiritually, we're not to be empty, but we are to live full. Rejoicing helps us refuel spiritually. To keep our joy level from getting low, we're to keep rejoicing – it will help us reach our destination.

Rejoicing isn't a feeling, but a decision. We aren't to have only moments of rejoicing, but a lifestyle of rejoicing. As Paul instructed, *"Rejoice in the Lord ALWAYS."*

First Peter 1:8 tells us, *"...yet BELIEVING, YE REJOICE with JOY unspeakable and full of glory."* When you're believing, you're rejoicing. To fall behind in rejoicing is to fall behind in exercising faith. To keep faith flowing, keep rejoicing, for rejoicing and praising hastens victory!

The Wells of Salvation

ISAIAH 12:2 & 3
2 Behold, God is my salvation; I will trust, and not be afraid: for the Lord Jehovah is my strength and my song; he also is become my salvation.

3 Therefore WITH JOY SHALL YE DRAW WATER OUT OF THE WELLS OF SALVATION.

Jesus declared, *"...the water that I shall give him shall be IN HIM A WELL OF WATER springing up into everlasting life"* (John 4:14). In your spirit is the well of salvation. Salvation is in you – it's in your spirit. W.E. Vine's *Expository Dictionary of New Testament Words* says that the word "salvation" sums up all the blessings bestowed by God on men in Christ through the Holy Spirit. God's blessings are in you. *"...The kingdom of God is within you"* (Luke 17:21). All the blessings belonging to the Kingdom of God are in you.

Ephesians 1:3 reads, *"Blessed be the God and Father of our Lord Jesus Christ, who HATH blessed us with all spiritual blessings in heavenly places in Christ...."* Another translation reads that God has blessed us with everything that "heaven itself enjoys."

Jesus spoke of rivers of living water that would flow from within, and He also spoke of wells of water that would spring up from within. These are two different flows, and they each have a different function.

In speaking about the rivers of living water, John 7:38 & 39 records that Jesus declared, *"He that believeth on me, as the scripture hath said, out of his belly shall flow RIVERS of living water. (But this spake he of the Spirit, which they that believe on him should receive: for the Holy Ghost was not yet given; because that Jesus was not yet glorified.)"*

Jesus was telling His disciples that once they received the Holy Spirit, there would flow out of their spirits rivers of living waters. Rivers flow. These rivers are to flow out of believers to others – to bless the lives of others.

In speaking about the well of water that springs up, Jesus declared, "*...the water that I shall give him shall be IN HIM a WELL of water SPRINGING up into everlasting life*" (John 4:14). The well of water that springs up from the spirit of the believer is to nourish his own life – that's what the believer is to drink from to water his own life.

How do you draw out and drink of that well that springs up from within? Isaiah 12:3 tells us that "with joy" we draw out of the wells of salvation. As you rejoice, thanking God for what He has made yours, you dip down into the waters of salvation and draw out the blessing of God within you.

What do you need? Healing, peace, power? Draw it out!

When you understand the wealth of blessings that are yours because you are in Christ and that they reside in your spirit – health, peace, victory, and all of salvation's blessings – and you begin to rejoice, thanking God that they are your present possession, then they will begin to spring up and flow into the different arenas of your life.

Rejoice in the riches of salvation within you and draw out the wealth of God's blessings from within.

Praising God Continually

HEBREWS 13:15
By him therefore let us offer the sacrifice of praise to God CONTINUALLY, that is, the fruit of our lips giving thanks to his name.

(AMPC)
Through Him, therefore, let us CONSTANTLY AND AT ALL TIMES offer up to God a sacrifice of praise, which is the fruit of lips that thankfully acknowledge and confess and glorify His name.

We are to offer the sacrifice of praise to God continually. What is the sacrifice of praise? It is the fruit of our lips giving thanks to His Name. We are to have a lifestyle of praising and thanking God continually, praising and thanking God for all His blessings and the benefits He has made ours – healing, prosperity, peace, guidance, and all that He has made ours. As we praise God and give Him thanks, it keeps us mindful of what's ours in Christ, and we keep the flow of those blessings active in our lives.

The Lord Has Done Great Things for Us

PSALM 126:1-3
1 When the Lord turned again the captivity of Zion, we were like them that dream.
2 Then was our mouth filled with LAUGHTER, and our tongue with SINGING: then said they among the heathen, The Lord hath done great things for them.

3 THE LORD HATH DONE GREAT THINGS FOR US; whereof we are GLAD.

The Lord has done great things for us! We were once held as captives, but Jesus freed us! Since we are free, our mouths are to be filled with laughter, singing, and gladness. These words, seen in the verses above, are expressions of joy and faith, and as they flow, God's power moves in our lives.

As you rejoice and praise God in the face of difficulties, it helps to keep your focus off the opposition and on God and His Word, which is your answer. It also holds you in the spirit arena, the arena of faith, and out of the mental arena.

No matter what the circumstances may be, you can laugh and rejoice, counting it a joy to stand on God's Word and again prove His faithfulness in your life. No matter what you may be feeling and seeing, continue to rejoice, for you know that the enemy is defeated and the victory is yours.

Make rejoicing part of your daily lifestyle, for that is the voice of living faith.

Chapter 12

A Disciplined Mind in Prayer

Not only will you have to discipline your mind to think in line with the Word in everyday life, but you will also have to discipline your mind while praying.

God has been teaching me and helping me to understand many of the things I have experienced in my prayer life. Although there is still much to learn, I include in this chapter some of the things I have learned to help bring understanding for those who may have experienced some of these same things. Although I won't go into an in-depth teaching, I do want to touch on these things to help bring clarity to this subject, for as we gain understanding along these lines, then we can better cooperate with the Spirit of God, and the enemy can't take advantage of us through the lack of knowledge.

As you build a prayer life that's based firmly on the Word, and as you are sensitive to follow the leading of the Spirit, your prayer life will bear much fruit and bless the lives of others.

However, the enemy doesn't want you to enter this prayer life, for as you cooperate with God in prayer, exercising your rights and authority, the enemy can't work his plan; therefore, he will oppose you in the great work of prayer. *As you pray, the enemy will send every kind of fiery dart against the mind, but these attacks come to try to distract you from the spirit; he's trying to hold you in the mental arena and out of the spirit arena, the arena of faith. Quench every fiery dart by holding up the shield of faith in God's Word.*

The enemy will send all kinds of thoughts, including accusing thoughts – thoughts that accuse you with your past, your sins, your faults, or your failures. He does this to try to weaken your stand of faith; he's trying to hold you in the mental arena and out of the spirit arena, which is the arena of faith. To stay in the arena of faith, a disciplined mind is necessary. You must cast down imaginations and thoughts that aren't in line with God's Word, answering every thought with the Word of God (2 Cor. 10:5), and then his attempts against you will be unsuccessful.

Never back down from moving with God in prayer, but take with you to prayer an accurate and clear understanding of the Word of God; judge all things in the light of His Word.

Casting Down Imaginations

When you pray in other tongues, the words come up from your spirit, not from your mind. Since speaking in other tongues bypasses and doesn't involve the mind, one of the enemy's strategies is to seek to distract your mind with all kinds of troubling or accusing thoughts while praying, but cast them down.

While praying in other tongues, quiet your mind and focus on your spirit. As you do, you will become more spirit-conscious and will more clearly perceive the leading of the Spirit of God.

Praying for Others

As you spend time praying in the Spirit, in other tongues, you may begin to sense the condition or needs of others; this can seem so real to you that you might think that what you are sensing actually pertains to you, but you are really sensing the condition or need of another. (If you don't understand this, the enemy may try to tell you that something is wrong with you; he may try to make you unsettled or fearful that what you are sensing is something pertaining to you, when it pertains to another. The enemy is trying to distract you out of faith, away from your spirit and into the mental arena, but stay in the spirit arena.) When you do sense the condition or the need of another, just continue to pray in the Spirit until the prayer burden lifts.

During Jesus' earthly ministry, we see His compassion for the people. He was moved with compassion for the sick and for those in need; His compassion brought deliverance (Matt. 14:14; Matt. 15:32; Matt. 20:34).

Hebrews 4:15 tells us, *"For we have not an high priest which cannot be touched with the FEELING of our infirmities...."* Jesus can be touched with the feeling of our infirmities, and when we move into divine compassion, we begin to feel like Jesus feels for another. Divine compassion feels as another feels. That's why we may actually sense the condition or needs of another. When we enter into that divine compassion in prayer, there will be deliverance.

While praying in the Spirit, in other tongues, I will sometimes have a sense of heaviness; what I am sensing pertains to someone else. I am sensing the Spirit within me reaching out to God on behalf of another. (When sensing this, it seems so real that you may think it pertains to you, but don't associate it with yourself.) I pray in other tongues until it lifts.

As I awake in the morning, I will sometimes have a sense of heaviness. (When first waking in the morning, the mind is less active, making it easier to perceive these spiritual things.) I just pray in other tongues until the burden lifts. When the burden lifts, then I know that that which I am praying for is dealt with. I am being a co-laborer with God on behalf of someone else or about something.

Sometimes during the day, my mind seems to become distracted, and I find it difficult to concentrate on the task at hand; I realize that either God wants to speak to me, or I am to pray for someone else or about something, so I begin to pray. I don't focus on the mental arena to try and figure out what I'm sensing, but I quiet my mind; I focus on my spirit and begin to pray in the Spirit, in other tongues. If I am to pray for someone else or about something, a spirit of prayer will begin to move within me. I continue to pray in other tongues until the burden of prayer lifts.

At times, when praying for someone who is facing a physical condition or is under mental pressure or heaviness, you may sense their need. It may seem in the spirit as though their condition is upon your own body or mind, but physically or literally it is not so; again, you are sensing their need in the spirit. Continue to pray in the Spirit until you sense that burden lift.

Keen in Discernment

How do you know whether the enemy is attacking your mind while praying or whether you are just sensing the condition of another? If the enemy is attacking your mind, the thoughts are coming against your mind from the outside. As you cast them down, quenching them with the shield of faith in God's Word, those thoughts will be overcome. If you are sensing the condition of another, that which you are sensing is rising up from within your spirit, and what you are sensing will continue; pray until that burden lifts. By quieting your mind and focusing on your spirit, you will be more keen in your discernment, and you'll be able to discern when you are sensing someone else's condition.

While praying, don't try to mentally figure out or mentally process these things you sense, and don't put your own interpretation on them, for they are spiritually discerned.

We won't always know who we're praying for or what we're praying about, for we don't always need to know. If we need to know, God will tell us; otherwise, we're to leave it with Him. We are to just yield to the Spirit as He leads us.

Groanings and Travail

Paul tells us in Romans,

ROMANS 8:26
Likewise the Spirit also helpeth our infirmities: for we know not what we should pray for as we ought: but the Spirit itself (Himself) **maketh intercession for us with GROANINGS which cannot be uttered.**

Paul also stated in Galatians 4:19, *"My little children, of whom I TRAVAIL in birth again until Christ be formed in you."* As a woman will groan and travail while in childbirth, you may experience similar things while praying for another.

Under that spirit of prayer, sometimes I sense groanings and even weeping rise up from my spirit, so I will groan until that lifts. Still other times, I have a strong urge to pray in other tongues, so I speak those utterances out. Groanings and tongues will often flow together, moving from one to the other. Yield to how the Spirit is leading you until that urge or burden lifts.

There have been times that I have sensed these things rise up within me for only a moment or for a longer period of time. I yielded to these leadings of the Spirit until the burden lifted.

Groaning or travailing in the Spirit is directed toward God, not the enemy, so realize that you're conducting business with God.

Praying for the Lost

When in a service where an altar call is given, there may be times that you sense such a burden of sin that you might think you need to answer the altar call yourself. But at those times, you are sensing the spiritual condition of a lost person. It can seem as though the burden of another person's sin is on your own conscience; you should simply pray quietly in other tongues until the burden lifts. If praying quietly is difficult, then go to a place where you can be alone to pray so that those around you won't be disturbed.

Prayer Armor

In chapter 3, I taught how we must be arrayed in our spiritual armor for daily life. (Review this portion in chapter 3.) But this is the armor that we must also be arrayed in before entering the prayer life. Paul describes our armor in Ephesians 6:13-17, and then in the very next verse he instructs us, *"Praying always with all prayer and supplication in the Spirit, and watching thereunto with all perseverance and supplication for all saints"* (Eph. 6:18). After listing our armor, he instructs us to pray for all saints; so, this armor is for our prayer life as well as for our daily life – it is prayer armor.

We are to be continually arrayed in our spiritual armor for daily life and for prayer. We are to put on the girdle of truth and the breastplate of righteousness, have our feet shod with the preparation of the gospel of peace, hold up the shield of faith, put on the helmet of salvation, and use the sword of the Spirit, which is the Word of God in our mouth (Eph. 6:13-17).

When praying, this spiritual armor is for our defense and protection against all the enemy's strategies and devices. When we are fully dressed in this armor, every device and strategy of the enemy against us will be unsuccessful.

By the Spirit

These different leadings and experiences in prayer happen by the Spirit and not by our own natural effort. The different ways the Spirit leads us will always be in line with God's Word, and as we are open and sensitive to the Spirit and cooperate with Him, our prayer lives will bear much fruit.

Chapter 13

Perfect Peace

Thou wilt keep him in PERFECT PEACE, whose mind is STAYED on thee: because he trusteth in thee.
– Isaiah 26:3

You will guard him and keep him in PERFECT and CONSTANT PEACE whose mind...is STAYED on You, because he commits himself to You, leans on You, and hopes confidently in You.
– Isaiah 26:3 (AMPC)

"*Thou wilt keep him in PERFECT PEACE....*" Perfect peace is continual peace, constant peace, and uninterrupted peace; this will be experienced by the person whose mind is stayed on God.

How do we keep our minds stayed on Him? God and His Word are one; we keep our minds stayed on Him by keeping our minds stayed on His Word – keeping our thoughts full of the Word. We are to meditate on His Word day and night, making it a lifestyle (Joshua 1:8).

For the one who keeps his mind stayed on the Word, God is able to hold him in perfect peace. But when someone allows his mind to be occupied with thoughts that are not in line with God's Word, God is not able to hold that man in perfect peace, for there is no perfect peace apart from the Word of God. He will have to return to the thoughts of the Word to return to perfect peace.

We must discipline our minds if we are to keep them stayed on Him. All kinds of situations and difficulties will arise in life, tempting us to draw our minds in the wrong direction. But as we cast down wrong thoughts, refusing to touch them in our thought life, as we bring every thought in line with God's Word, and as we stay in the arena of faith by refusing to worry, fear, or doubt, those temptations will be successfully resisted. When surrounded by unfavorable circumstances and when faced with opposition, we will be undisturbed and held in perfect peace as we keep our thoughts and attention on His Word.

As we daily renew our minds, we will become more proficient at keeping them stayed on God's Word in the face of opposition, and the result will be perfect peace.

Peace doesn't mean the absence of opposition, but peace means you refuse to be disturbed or unsettled in the face of opposition, for you choose to believe God's Word and to hold fast to it in all situations and under all circumstances. You can be peaceful no matter what the situation, for you know you've been raised and seated with Christ in heavenly places and that all opposition is under your feet – you are *far above* it all!

Multiplied Peace

2 PETER 1:2
Grace and PEACE BE MULTIPLIED unto you through the KNOWLEDGE of God, and of Jesus our Lord.

(AMPC)
May grace (God's favor) and PEACE (which is perfect well-being, all necessary good, all spiritual prosperity, and freedom from fears and agitating passions and moral conflicts) BE MULTIPLIED to you in [the full, personal, precise, and CORRECT] KNOWLEDGE of God and of Jesus our Lord.

As you grow in the correct knowledge of God's Word, so does your peace – your peace is multiplied. As you gain knowledge of God's Word and act on that Word, your mind becomes renewed, and the result is peace.

As you see your all-conquering position in Christ and take your place in Christ, exercising your God-given authority, you will reign in life over all circumstances, and peace will be your flow.

Continue to renew your mind day by day with the Word of God, discipline your thought life to think in line with the Word of God, and be a doer of the Word, for the Word won't leave you like it found you – it will transform you!

Prayer of Salvation

Heavenly Father, I come to You in the Name of Jesus. Your Word says, *"...him that cometh to me I will in no wise cast out"* (John 6:37). So I know You won't cast me out, but You will take me in, and I thank You for it.

You said in Your Word, *"...If thou shalt confess with thy mouth the Lord Jesus, and shalt believe in thine heart that God hath raised him from the dead, thou shalt be saved. For whosoever shall call upon the name of the Lord shall be saved"* (Rom. 10:9 & 13).

I believe in my heart that Jesus Christ is the Son of God. I believe Jesus died for my sins and was raised from the dead so I can be in right-standing with God. I am calling upon His Name, the Name of Jesus, so I know, Father, that You save me now.

Your Word says, *"...with the heart man believeth unto righteousness; and with the mouth confession is made unto salvation"* (Rom. 10:10). I do believe with my heart, and I confess Jesus now as my Lord. Therefore, I am saved! Thank You, Father.

Please write us and let us know that you have just been born again. When you write, ask to receive our salvation booklets.

To contact us, please email us at
dm@dufresneministries.org
or write to:
Dufresne Ministries
P.O. Box 1010
Murrieta, CA 92564

How To Be Filled With the Holy Spirit

Acts 2:38 reads, *"...Repent, and be baptized every one of you in the name of Jesus Christ for the remission of sins, and ye shall receive the GIFT of the Holy Ghost."* The Holy Ghost is a gift that belongs to each one of God's people. Jesus is the gift God gave the whole world, but the Holy Spirit is a gift that belongs only to God's people.

Jesus told His disciples, *"But ye shall receive POWER, after that the Holy Ghost is come upon you: and ye shall be witnesses unto me..."* (Acts 1:8). When you're baptized with the Holy Spirit, you receive supernatural power that enables you to live victoriously.

Indwelling vs. Infilling

When you're born again, you receive the indwelling of the Person of the Holy Spirit. Romans 8:16 tells us, *"The Spirit itself* (Himself) *beareth witness with our spirit, that we are the children of God."* When you're born again, you know it because the Spirit bears witness with your own spirit that you are a child of God; He confirms it to you. He's able to bear witness with your spirit because He's in you; you are *indwelt* by the Spirit of God.

But the Word of God speaks of another experience subsequent to the new birth that belongs to every believer, and that is to be baptized with the Holy Spirit, or to receive the *infilling* of the Holy Spirit.

God wants you to be full and overflowing with the Spirit. Being filled with the Spirit is likened to being full of water. Just because you had one drink of water doesn't mean you're full of water. At the new birth, you received the indwelling of the Spirit – a drink of water. But now God wants you to be filled to overflowing – be filled with His Spirit, baptized with the Holy Ghost.

> **ACTS 2:1-4**
> **1 And when the day of Pentecost was fully come, they were all with one accord in one place.**
> **2 And suddenly there came a sound from heaven as of a rushing mighty wind, and it filled all the house where they were sitting.**
> **3 And there appeared unto them cloven tongues like as of fire, and it sat upon each of them.**
> **4 And they were all FILLED with the Holy Ghost, and BEGAN TO SPEAK WITH OTHER TONGUES, as the Spirit gave them utterance.**

When these disciples were filled with the Holy Ghost, they began to speak with other tongues as the Spirit gave them utterance; they spoke in a language unknown to them. Today, when a believer is filled with the Holy Ghost, they will speak with other tongues too. These are not words that come from the mind of man, but they are words given by the Holy Spirit; these words float up from their spirit within, and the person then speaks those out.

What is the benefit of being filled with the Holy Ghost with the evidence of speaking in other tongues? First Corinthians 14:2 reads, *"For he that speaketh in an unknown tongue speaketh not unto men, but unto God...."* When you're speaking in other tongues, you're speaking to God – it is a divine means of communicating with your Heavenly Father. This is one of many great benefits.

> **MATTHEW 7:7-11**
> **7 Ask, and it shall be given you...**
> **8 FOR EVERY ONE THAT ASKETH RECEIVETH...**
> **9 ...what man is there of you, whom if his son ask bread, will he give him a stone?**
> **10 Or if he ask a fish, will he give him a serpent?**
> **11 If ye then, being evil, know how to give good gifts unto your children, HOW MUCH MORE SHALL YOUR FATHER WHICH IS IN HEAVEN GIVE GOOD THINGS TO THEM THAT ASK HIM?**

In this passage, Jesus is saying that when you ask God for something, you shall receive it! Believe that He will give you that which you ask for. When you ask God for something good, He won't give you something that will harm you; He will give you the good thing you ask for. The baptism of the Holy Spirit is a good gift, and when you ask God to fill you with the Holy Spirit, you won't receive a wrong spirit; you will receive this good gift, the gift of the Holy Spirit.

Once you receive the gift of the Holy Ghost, you can yield to this gift any time, speaking in other tongues as often as you choose; you don't have to wait for God to move on you. The more you speak in other tongues, the more you will benefit from this gift. By continuing to speak in other tongues on a daily basis, you will be able to maintain a Spirit-filled life; you will live full of the Spirit.

The more you take time to speak in other tongues, the deeper you'll move into the things of God.

(For more teaching on being filled with the Holy Spirit, I recommend the mini-book, *Why Tongues?* by Kenneth E. Hagin.)

Prayer To Receive the Holy Spirit

"Father, I see that the gift of the Holy Spirit belongs to Your children. So, I come to You to receive this gift. I received my salvation by faith, so I receive the gift of the Holy Spirit by faith. I believe I receive the Holy Spirit now! Since I'm filled with the Holy Spirit now, I expect to speak in other tongues as the Spirit gives me utterance, just like those in Acts 2 on the Day of Pentecost. Thank You for filling me with the Holy Ghost."

Now, words that the Spirit of God gives you will float up from your spirit. You are the one who must open your mouth and speak those words out. The words will not come to your mind, but they will float up from your spirit. Speak those out freely.